CAMBRIDGE LIBRARY COLLECTION

Books of enduring scholarly value

Egyptology

The large-scale scientific investigation of Egyptian antiquities by Western scholars began as an unintended consequence of Napoleon's invasion of Egypt during which, in 1799, the Rosetta Stone was discovered. The military expedition was accompanied by French scholars, whose reports prompted a wave of enthusiasm that swept across Europe and North America resulting in the Egyptian Revival style in art and architecture. Increasing numbers of tourists visited Egypt, eager to see the marvels being revealed by archaeological excavation. Writers and booksellers responded to this growing interest with publications ranging from technical site reports to tourist guidebooks and from children's histories to theories identifying the pyramids as repositories of esoteric knowledge. This series reissues a wide selection of such books. They reveal the gradual change from the 'tomb-robbing' approach of early excavators to the highly organised and systematic approach of Flinders Petrie, the 'father of Egyptology', and include early accounts of the decipherment of the hieroglyphic script.

Abydos

A pioneering Egyptologist, Sir William Matthew Flinders Petrie (1853–1942) excavated over fifty sites and trained a generation of archaeologists. Originally published between 1902 and 1904 for the Egypt Exploration Fund, this three-volume set of reports documents the excavations that Petrie initiated at one of ancient Egypt's most sacred sites, the necropolis at Abydos. These reports follow on from the findings published in *The Royal Tombs of the First Dynasty* (1900) and *The Royal Tombs of the Earliest Dynasties* (1901), both of which are reissued in this series. Volume 1 presents a detailed account of the objects found in the Osiris *temenos* (enclosure) and the cemetery known as 'G' during the dig of 1902. Eighty pages of plates illustrate the discoveries, which range from painted pottery to early dynastic graves. A chapter by Arthur Weigall (1880–1934) sheds light on the inscriptions.

Abydos

Volume 1

W.M. Flinders Petrie

CAMBRIDGE
UNIVERSITY PRESS

CAMBRIDGE
UNIVERSITY PRESS

University Printing House, Cambridge, CB2 8BS, United Kingdom

Published in the United States of America by Cambridge University Press, New York

Cambridge University Press is part of the University of Cambridge.
It furthers the University's mission by disseminating knowledge in the pursuit of
education, learning and research at the highest international levels of excellence.

www.cambridge.org
Information on this title: www.cambridge.org/9781108061292

© in this compilation Cambridge University Press 2013

This edition first published 1902
This digitally printed version 2013

ISBN 978-1-108-06129-2 Paperback

This book reproduces the text of the original edition. The content and language reflect
the beliefs, practices and terminology of their time, and have not been updated.

Cambridge University Press wishes to make clear that the book, unless originally published
by Cambridge, is not being republished by, in association or collaboration with, or
with the endorsement or approval of, the original publisher or its successors in title.

ABYDOS

PART I. 1902

BY

W. M. FLINDERS PETRIE

Hon. D.C.L., LL.D., Litt.D., Ph.D.,
F.R.S., Hon. F.S.A. (Scot.)

MEMBER OF THE IMPERIAL GERMAN ARCHAEOLOGICAL INSTITUTE;
CORRESPONDING MEMBER OF THE SOCIETY OF ANTHROPOLOGY, BERLIN;
MEMBER OF THE ROMAN SOCIETY OF ANTHROPOLOGY;
MEMBER OF THE SOCIETY OF NORTHERN ANTIQUARIES;
EDWARDS PROFESSOR OF EGYPTOLOGY, UNIVERSITY COLLEGE, LONDON.

With Chapter by

A. E. WEIGALL

TWENTY-SECOND MEMOIR OF

THE EGYPT EXPLORATION FUND

PUBLISHED BY ORDER OF THE COMMITTEE

LONDON
SOLD AT
The OFFICES OF THE EGYPT EXPLORATION FUND, 37, Great Russell Street, W.C.
and 59, Temple Street, Boston, Mass., U.S.A.
and by KEGAN PAUL, TRENCH, TRÜBNER & CO., Paternoster House, Charing Cross Road, W.C.
B. QUARITCH, 15, Piccadilly, W.; ASHER & CO., 13, Bedford Street, Covent Garden, W.C.
and HENRY FROWDE, Amen Corner, E.C.

1902

LONDON :
PRINTED BY GILBERT AND RIVINGTON, LTD.
ST. JOHN'S HOUSE, CLERKENWELL.

AAHMES.

AMENHOTEP.   AAHMES.

CONTENTS.

INTRODUCTION.

SECT.   PAGE
1. Scope of the excavations . . . 1
2. The work and workers . . . 1

CHAPTER I.
OBJECTS FROM THE ROYAL TOMBS.

3. King Ka. Pls. i–iii 3
4. King Ro. Pl. iii 4
5. Small inscriptions. Pls. iv–v . . 5
6. The pottery. Pls. vi–vii . . . 6
7. The Aegean pottery. Pl. viii . . 6
8. The stone vases. Pls. ix, x . . 7
9. The labels, &c. Pls. xi, xii . . 7
10. The steles, &c. Pl. xiii . . . 7
11. The flints. Pls. xiv, xv . . . 8

CHAPTER II.
THE OSIRIS TEMENOS.

12. Character of the site 9
13. The early town. 9
14. The flints. Pls. xvi–xxvi. . . 10
15. The stone vases. Pl. xxvii . . 12
16. The pottery. Pls. xxviii–xxxv . 12
17. The M. tombs 14
18. The plans of M tombs. Pls. xlviii,
    xlix 15
19. The pottery and stone. Pls. xxxvi–
    xlvii 18
20. The date of the town and tombs . 19
21. The slates and tools. Pl. l . . 23
22. The amulets, &c. Pls. li–liii . . 23

CHAPTER III.
THE OSIRIS TEMPLE.

SECT.   PAGE
23. Position and history 27
24. Before the XIIth Dynasty. Pls. liv–
    lvii 27
25. XIIth and XIIIth Dynasty. Pls. lviii–
    lx 28
26. The XVIIIth Dynasty. Pls. lxi–lxiv 29
27. The XIXth Dynasty. Pls. lxv–lxvii. 31
28. The XXVIth Dynasty, and later.
    Pls. lxviii–lxx 31

CHAPTER IV.
THE CEMETERY G.

29. Range of the cemetery . . . 34
30. Early tombs 35
31. Tomb G. 57. Pls. lxxii, lxxiv . . 35
32. Construction of the later tombs . 36
33. Tomb of Zedher. Pls. lxxv, lxxix . 37
34. Other tombs 39

CHAPTER V.
THE INSCRIPTIONS.
BY A. E. WEIGALL.

35. Monuments of VIth–XIth Dynasty . 41
36. The XIIth and XIIIth Dynasty . 42
37. The XVIIIth and XIXth Dynasty . 43
38. Monuments of Un-nefer . . . 46
39. The XXVIth and XXVIIIth Dynasty 48
40. Sarcophagi, XXXth Dynasty . . 48
41. The hypocephali 49
42. Inscriptions not figured . . . 51

LIST OF PLATES.

PLATE		PAGE
Frontispiece.	Heads of Aahmes I and Amenhotep I, royal tombs	30
I	Jars of King Ka—Ap.	3
II	„ „	3
III	„ „ and Queen Ha, &c.	3
IV	Inscriptions, Sma to Zet	5
V	„ Azab to Qa	5
VI	Pottery, to Zer	6
VII	„ Den to Khasekhemui	6
VIII	„ from Aegean	6
IX	Stone vases	7
X	Alabaster vases, &c.	7
XI	Ivory and ebony labels	7
XII	Marks on stone vases	7
XIII	Steles and gold bar	7
XIV	Flints, to Den	8
XV	Flints, Azab to end	8

Osiris Temenos.

XVI, XVII	Flint knives without handles	10
XVIII, XIX	Flint knives with handles	11
XX	Flint hoes	11
XXI	Tailed scrapers	11
XXII	Irregular scrapers	11
XXIII	Round scrapers	11
XXIV	Long scrapers and flakes	11
XXV	Wrought flakes	12
XXVI	Animal flints, saws, crescents and combs	12
XXVII	Stone vases	12
XXVIII—XXXV	Early pottery	12-14
XXXVI—XLI	Pottery of M. tombs	18
XLII—XLVII	Stone vases of M. tombs	18
XLVIII, XLIX	Plans of M. tombs	15-18
L	Painted pottery, slates, tools, marks	23

PLATE		PAGE
LI	Amulets &c.	23
LII	Beads, whorls, &c.	24
LIII	Fire places, tiles, grinders, &c.	25
LIV	Inscriptions of VIth Dynasty,	27-41
LV	Inscriptions IVth—XIIth Dynasty	27, 41
LVI	Columns of Antef V	28, 41
LVII	Stele of Nekht	28, 41
LVIII	Inscription of UsertesenI	28, 42
LIX	Inscription of XIIIth Dynasty	29, 42
LX	Inscription of XIIIth Dynasty	29, 42
LXI	Inscription of XVIIIth Dynasty	30
LXII, LXIII	Sculptures of Amenhotep I	30, 43
LXIV	Inscription of Tahutmes II & III	30, 43
LXV	Inscriptions of XIXth Dynasty	31, 44
LXVI	Inscriptions of XVIIIth — XIXth Dynasty	31, 44
LXVII	Inscriptions of Ptahemua, &c.	31, 45
LXVIII	Shrine of Haa-ab-ra	32
LXIX	Altars of XXVIth Dynasty	32, 48
LXX	Bronzes, foundation deposits, &c.	32

Cemetery G.

LXXI	Coffin of Tahutimes	35, 48
LXXII	Box, &c., of Mertiu-heru	35, 48
LXXIII	Coffin inscriptions	35, 48
LXXIV	Canopic boxes, &c.	35, 48
LXXV	Sarcophagi inscriptions	39, 49
LXXVI	Hypocephalus, G. 50, B	38, 49
LXXVII	Hypocephali G. 50, c, D	38, 49
LXXVIII	Amulets	38
LXXIX	Ushabtis, &c.	38, 39
LXXX	Sections and plans of tombs	15-17, 34-40

ABYDOS I.

INTRODUCTION.

1. The present volume completes the account of the objects found in the Royal Tombs of the earliest dynasties, the discoveries in which during the previous two years have appeared in the last two volumes. The account of the results of the present year's excavations covers nearly all that has been yet found in the Temenos of Osiris and the well-known cemetery; but another large part of our work is kept back for publication when completed next year. It is always difficult to decide between partial publication in sections, issued rapidly for the immediate benefit of scholars, and systematic publication delayed until every detail has been finally sifted and settled. But the worst of the bulletin system is that the student is afterwards dependent on indexes to find connected subjects; while the worst of the great book long delayed is that often the material loses value while waiting, and the delays may run on so that much is forgotten in the interval.

The Temenos of Osiris I had wished to excavate since I first saw it in 1887. It was undoubtedly one of the oldest centres of worship, and had a long history to be unravelled. If it has proved so far rather different to what was expected, it the more corrects our ideas. But the real temple site has not yet been touched below the level of the XVIIIth Dynasty; and a vast deal still remains to be done there.

The cemetery G was only worked as proved desirable in intervals of other work, and to give employment to workmen between other enterprises. Lying close behind our huts, and with scarcely any small objects of value casually found in it, such a place was an ideal resort whenever men could not be kept on elsewhere. I should hardly have worked it for its own sake alone; but as a stop-gap it proved very convenient, and fairly desirable.

The other large work, which is not described at all in this volume, occupied half of our men, or more, all the season. About a mile south of Abydos, at the foot of the desert cliffs, I had noticed some great tombs when first visiting the ground. The temple which Mr. MacIver excavated two years ago (see the volume on *El Amrah* just issued) proved to belong to a king Kha-kau-ra, presumably Usertesen III., but possibly of a king of the XIIIth Dynasty. The temple lies on the edge of the desert, and a long causeway leads up to one of the great tombs which we have found. As probably most of next season's work will be occupied with these tombs, before they are finally cleared, it is best to leave aside the plans which have been prepared, and give a connected account of the whole site next year.

2. Our excavators were the same gang of men and boys from Koptos who have worked for me during many years. Indeed that gang

B

has served as a nucleus for all other recent excavators, as Dr. Reisner, at Girgeh, has drawn almost entirely on that centre, and the German work at Abusir has used our trained Quftis for headmen, to say nothing of the Research Account work at El Kab, which has depended on the same source. I have no doubt other places would furnish equally desirable workers, but when once a large party have been trained, they are naturally sought for elsewhere. It is needful, however, to carry on a continual weeding of old hands, as the Egyptian always becomes spoiled with prosperity; and some of the boys, as they have grown up, have come to the front line in their intelligence and conduct. We also employed over a hundred boys, from villages near the work, to do the carrying.

Our camp was entirely fresh, as those who were with us before had all passed on to other work. Mr. Arthur Weigall came out for the first time, and proved a most successful worker. I greatly regret, for the sake of our work, that I have to congratulate him on passing on at once to a better position. He entirely superintended the men at the great southern tombs, which I only visited to give general direction to the region of work. He also looked after the close of the temenos work, and drew some of the inscriptions, the whole of which he comments on in this volume. Mr. Laurence Christie, who came for artistic copying, has done more than four plates in this volume; but most of his time was given to copying selected sculptures in the Sety temple for the Research Account. Excavations at the Sety temple, on the same basis, were carried on by Mr. A. St. G. Caulfeild, who also took many photographs, some of which appear in this frontispiece. My wife was closely occupied with drawing nearly all the season; especially on the tedious figuring of nearly four hundred flints, and the exact facsimile copies of inscriptions. My own work lay in the Temenos of Osiris, directing the diggers, levelling and recording, and general management and account keeping; for the season's work involves some 40,000 entries of small sums. I have also drawn thirty-seven of the plates here, and taken the photographs. The immediate production of a fully-illustrated bulletin of the results of a season, before the objects reach England, involves organizing all the copying on the spot; but the advantages of quick publication make it well worth while to carry out this system, as we have now done for three years.

CHAPTER I.

OBJECTS FROM THE ROYAL TOMBS.

3. The earliest royal tomb that can yet be placed in the series is that of king Ka, which was described in the last volume (*Royal Tombs*, ii, p. 7). Within the chamber were hundreds of fragments of cylindrical jars (type, pl. vi, 1), some of them with cross-lined pattern copied from cordage. Such jars are well known in the later prehistoric pottery, and belong to the sequence date 78 in that scale. On many of these jars are inscriptions, roughly written in ink with a brush; and on comparing all of the fragments, I have succeeded in putting together those which are copied in plates i., ii., and iii. They prove to be all of two formulae, one for the king, and one for his queen. And as being the oldest hieroglyphic inscriptions known, probably half-way back in the dynasty before Mena, they deserve our closest attention; they show the oldest shapes of the signs, and prove that at that age writing was so familiar that a rapid form of it was freely used to write on dozens of common pottery jars.

On plates i. and ii. it is seen that the whole formula was *Suten Ap*, the Horus *Ka*, followed by three strokes; and on plate iii. the second formula was *Ha hemt en* Horus *Ka*. Thus, as clearly as possible, these jars are inscribed for the king Ap, whose Horus name is Ka, and for Ha, the wife of the Horus Ka. The name Ap occurs as a masculine name in the Old Kingdom, and also very commonly the form Apa: while Hay and Hayt are known as feminine names. No objection has been made to this reading, even by those who are most surprised by such grammatical writing at that age. The meaning of the three strokes below the Horus name is not clear, and probably we shall have to wait for some better drawn inscription to explain them, as writing was so familiar to the scribe that mere indications were then enough to give the idea. There is no parallel to this group following any of the other early Horus names; and, as *maa kheru* and *neb taui* both belong to far later times, we may perhaps suppose these lines to represent some steps on which the funereal stele was erected, as on the alabaster of Azab, pl. v, or the pottery marks, probably all from Azab, in *Royal Tombs*, i, pl. xlvi, 111—155. The signs themselves show more than is yet known about them. Observe especially the *suten* plant, which is sometimes of the later normal form, as in Nos. 4, 7, and 9; more generally it has the leaf or flower at the top like the *qema* or *res* sign of the south; and generally the root is shown as a wavy line hanging from it, see especially Nos. 1, 2, 17, 19. This plant was then separate from the *nen* or *nekheb* plant, but no distinction between the *suten* and *qema* plant was yet made. Probably the use of this plant for *qema* or south was then in the stage of naming *the kingdom, par excellence*, before any other region to the north had been formally included in it: much as we should at present mean the British Isles by speaking of "the kingdom," in contrast to the far larger parts of the present kingdom in other regions.

The inversion of the form of the Horus- or *ka*-name is strange. That the strokes above the arms represent a panelling, like that placed below the name in all later examples, seems proved by their great variety, having any number of lines from two (fig. 5) to five (figs. 4, 20, 23), or even thirteen strokes scratched on pottery (*R. T.* ii, xiii); such could hardly be a hieroglyph. From later instances this panelling certainly is copied from the front of a building, tomb, or palace : so here we must take it as such, and see the space below it, which contains the sign, as equivalent to the doorway of the building. The instances scratched on pottery (*R. T.* ii, pl. xiii) should probably all be turned, with the *ka* arms upwards, and the panel strokes above them. It is evident that the position of the panelling strokes was changed between the time of Ka and that of Narmer.

The reed *a* has here the separate flowers of the feathery head, as in all early examples; but they vary from three to five in number. The mat-work *p* has the ends all left loose, as in the seals Nos. 16, 57-60, 72, 118, 160 (*R. T.* i, and ii.). The plant *ha* is like that on the Aha ebony tablet in having no base line (*R. T.* ii, x, 2); but the base line came in at that time, as on the tablet *R. T.* ii, pl. iii, 4, and perhaps the same on the tablet No. 3 in the same plate. The signs *hem* and *n* might belong to almost any later age.

Thus on the whole there are but two points in which a change took place between the signs of king Ka and the general usage of two or three centuries later; the *suten* sign passed into two distinct forms, those for "king" and "south," a political change hardly due to hieroglyphic development, and the *ka* name passed from the doorway of the panelling to the space over the panels. Neither of these changes are due to immaturity in the writing; and when we thus reach back a couple of centuries before Mena without finding any marked difference, and meet with a cursive writing, it is plain that we are very far from touching the period of its formation.

Beside the ink writing three more examples of incised writing of this same king are given, similar to those already published (*R. T.* ii, pl. xiii). On pl. iii, M 36 shows the tail of the hawk, part of the *ka* arms, and the top of the *suten*; 37 shows the *ka* arms and a sign near by which is probably a star and crescent mark like No. 605, &c. (*R. T.* i, pl. li); 38 shows that in one case, at least, the panel strokes were put below and the arms hang down, as the *suten* sign unquestionably shows which way up this is.

We may here briefly note the remaining figures in pl. iii. Nos. 39—43 are all numerical signs neatly painted in ink on alabaster jars, 39 from the tomb of king Den, 40—43 from the tomb of king Mersekha, but perhaps thrown over from Den or elsewhere. 44, 46, and 47 are ink writings on stone vases. 45 is ink writing on a jar from the tomb of Den; it reads *sesh*, and should be compared with other writing on vases *R. T.* i, pl. xxxii, 34 — 37; pl. xlii, 57—64; *R. T.* ii, pl. xxv, 13 — 27. The figure of the god Min (48), ink-drawn on a piece of slate bowl from the tomb of Khasekhemui, is the oldest drawn figure of that god. The signs on 49 are from a slate bowl of Perabsen.

4. When last year the names of the earliest kings were grouped together in *Royal Tombs*, vol. ii., I did not observe the presence of another name until the publication of the volume. On *R. T.* ii, pl. xiii, is a sealing No. 96, of which several fragments were found; this shows the hawk on the mouth hieroglyph. Again, on *R. T.* i, pl. xliv, there are several examples (Nos. 2 to 8) of what seems to be the same group. Considering that this group is thus formally cut on a seal, and often drawn on pottery, I think we are justified in seeing in it the royal hawk and the hieroglyph *r* or *ro*, expressing the *ka* name of a king, Ro. All of the pottery examples come from the tomb B 1, which, with B 2, was worked by Mr. MacIver in the first year; and this accords with their giving the name of a king, incised like the other early

kings' names, Ka (pl. iii, 38, &c.) and Nar (*R. T.* i, pl. xliv, 1), and belonging to the tomb of the king. These tombs B 1 and 2 are shown on the plan (*R. T.* ii, pl. lviii) immediately above the name BENER-AB.

The age of this king Ro cannot be far from that of king Ka. The position of the tomb does not indicate whether it was before or after that of Ka. But we must observe the presence of a great jar (*R. T.* i, pl. xxxix, 2), which is usual later, but does not occur in the tomb of Ka; the style of the sealing, which is more like those of Narmer or Mena than like the very simple one known of Ka (No. 89); and the clay, which is yellow marl (*heyb* Arab.) like later sealings, and not black mud like the Ka sealing. All of these details point to the order of the kings being—

KA
RO
ZESER
NARMER
SMA

before the Ist Dynasty opens with Aha—Mena. Thus we can now tolerably restore half of even the ten kings who reigned at Abydos before the united kingdom was established. The list on p. viii of *R. T.* ii, should be thus amended.

5. Some small inscribed objects were not photographed till they reached England, so could not be included in the previous volume. They are here given on pl. iv. Figs. 1 and 2 are pieces of crystal and syenite cups bearing the name of king Sma; by careful wiping with colour the hieroglyphs *nebui Sma* are here brought out visible. Fig. 3 is a piece of ivory bracelet, which was found in the tomb B 2 by Mr. MacIver; I then supposed that it might bear the name of Aha, and in the next season the objects of Benerab clearly showed that this was one of her bracelets, with her name and that of Aha, which had strayed over from the neighbouring tomb. Fig. 4 is a fragment of a

volcanic stone bowl from the tomb of Khasekhemui. Fig. 5 is a piece of an upright cup of pink limestone, with part of a strange hieroglyph upon it which we have not met with elsewhere; it might possibly be the base of a *ka* name, but the crosses below are unexplained. Fig. 6 is a piece of alabaster vase, with a faint inscription of Neithotep. Fig. 7 is the plait of hair and piece of false fringe found in the tomb of king Zer, probably belonging to his queen, on whose arm the bracelets were found: the fringe of locks is exquisitely made, entirely on a band of hair, showing a long acquaintance with hair-work at that age. It is now in the Pitt-Rivers Museum at Oxford. Fig. 8 is an inscription on a fragment of pottery vase from the tomb of king Zer. Fig. 9 is a piece of black pottery with incised patterns, belonging to the large class of such pottery known in the pre-historic age, the IIIrd and IVth Dynasties and the XIIth and XIIIth Dynasties (see *Naqada*, xxx; *Dendereh*, xxi, 1; *Kahun*, xxvii, 199—202; *Diospolis Parva*, xl, 43). The place of manufacture of this pottery is yet unknown, but it is wide-spread in the Mediterranean, as we have noticed before. Fig. 10 is the edge of a bowl of quartzose metamorphosed slate; on it is carved in relief the triple twist pattern. It is accidentally inverted here, and therefore reversed in lighting. Fig. 11 is a spirited drawing of a dwarf, outlined on a bowl of metamorphic rock. Fig. 12 is a piece of ivory, shown also in drawing on xi, 2; fig. 13 a piece of ivory, with a row of heads in squares, from the tomb of Zet; fig. 14 a piece of alabaster vase from the W tombs, probably of the reign of Zet.

Plate v. The fragments of an alabaster inscription of Azab were published separately before; for it was not till they came to England that I observed that the pieces fitted together, as they were found scattered in three different tombs. The inscription of Qa was found accidentally after publishing the others from that tomb. The gold foil of Qa seems to have been part of a model mat of a *hotep* offering, like that found at Hierakonpolis (*Hierakonpolis*, i, pl. xx, 9). The great stele of king Qa was found on the east side of his tomb as described (*R. T.* i, p. 15); the lower part of it had been removed by the *Mission Amélineau*, and was kept at the Cairo Museum; thence it has now been exchanged, and will rejoin the upper part in the Philadelphia Museum.

6. The pottery from the Royal Tombs is given on pls. vi, vii, in addition to that already published in *R. T.* i, pls. xxxix—xliii. It is here classed according to the period; and the following references are given to the volumes *Royal Tombs*, i (*R.*), and the present *Abydos* (*A.*), with the number of the pottery drawing in each. The large jars begin under king Ro with two bands and a bottom ring of rope pattern (*R.* 2); then pass on to plain bands, under Zer (*A.* 13); next the bands come closer together, under Mersekha (*R.* 6); further on they pass up to above the shoulder (*R.* 7), or dwindle to a single band, under Qa (*R.* 5); and lastly we see the jar far smaller with a single band, under Perabsen (*A.* 31).

Some curious late variants of the wavy-handled jars come from the tomb of Mena, B. 19. They are very thick, and so differ from the earlier types, though the form *A.* 3 is like that found far earlier; the arched pattern around it is, however, certainly late. The other forms, *A.* 5, 6, are more than half solid, and the arch pattern has sunk to two curves, or merely three finger pits. Later on under Zer, *A.* 15, 16, these become even more formalized; but it is curious that two different forms, this one and the cylinder jar, *A.* 1, 11, 12, were both derived from one prototype. It is explained, however, by the cylinder jar being a form influenced by approximating to the alabaster cylinder jars, which were already long in use (*Diospolis Parva*, p. 15, pl. iii); and the forms here, *A.* 3, 5, 6, 14, 15, 16; .*R.* 111—

114, must be looked on as the real close of the wavy-handled type.

The survival of black-topped pottery, *A.* 9, 10, under Zer is unexpected, as few forms last beyond 60, and scarcely any after 70, sequence date. These, however, are very different in appearance to the earlier black-topped, and are of forms unknown in the prehistoric; only the accidental blacking beneath the ashes resembles the early ware. The oval dishes, *A.* 19, 20, are the last descendants of the oval forms so usual in the early prehistoric; and no later examples than these have been found.

On reaching Perabsen we find the links to the regular forms of the Old Kingdom. The form *A.* 28, probably derived from that of Mena's age, *R.* 110, is the parent of the type of the VIth Dynasty (*Dendereh*, xvi. 5, 7, 22). The hand-made pot with diagonal finger marks, *A.* 27, is the parent of the usual pot of the IIIrd—IVth Dynasty (*Medum*, xxxi, 15); which in another variety (*Medum*, xxxi, 19) lasted on to the VIth Dynasty (*Dendereh*, xvi, 8).

The large limestone bowl, *A.* 33, found in the tomb of Mena, is like that of which a piece bears the name of Zet (*R. T.* ii, pl. vii, 2). The huge pilgrim-bottle, *A.* 34, is probably of the XXIInd Dynasty.

7. The Aegean pottery here figured, pl. viii. 1—14, was found together in a single deposit in the tomb of Zer, as described in detail in *Royal Tombs*, ii, pp. 9, 46; the account already given should be referred to, and we need only here say that the date and the foreign origin of this group are beyond question. Some regular Egyptian forms, such as 9, 10, 13, 14, and the alabaster 11, were deposited with the foreign forms, and show by the contrast the wide difference between them. The painted pieces below are from the tombs of Den (T) and Mersekha (U); the zigzag line between parallels is a well-known later design, but not hitherto met with in this age.

8. On plate ix are some outlines of stone vases, supplementary to those given in *Royal Tombs*, ii, pls. xlvi—liii. Fig. 1 is a portion of a syenite cup of king Sma, the inscription of which is here shown in photograph on pl. iv. 2. The very curious rush tray carved in alabaster, fig. 4, is here restored from fragments which were found scattered far apart. It is most like some of the remarkable slate carvings which have yet to be published, when the portions now hidden in Paris are available for science. The dolomite marble vases, figs. 5, 6, 7, 10, are those with gold caps, already published in photographs (*R. T.* ii, pl. ix, 2—10). Figs. 8, 9, were found with the copper bowls (*R. T.* ii, pl. ix, 13, 15). The diorite bowl, fig. 13, is photographed in *R. T.* ii, pl. ix, 11; for the position see *R. T.* ii, p. 13, chamber 44. The bowls, figs. 14, 15, are mentioned in position in *R. T.* ii, p. 12, chamber 16.

On plate x. is shown a small group found in the chamber Z 11, south of the tomb of king Zet. The zig-zag pattern, fig. 16, is incised on a bird's leg-bone, which probably served to hold copper needles; the copper borer, 19, is quadrangular; the two flint scrapers should be compared with those from Z on pl. xiv. Fig. 20 is a portion of a carved wooden tray, much weathered, but apparently of a close-grained conifer, probably cedar; the base is shown in the sketch, and part of the curved side. Fig. 21 is from a broken cup of thin horn, found in the tomb of Mena. The rude vases of alabaster are selected to show the variety of forms among the great number found in the tomb of Khasekhemui; the depth of the hollow is shown by a dotted line; these were drawn by Mr. Weigall.

9. As it was impossible to draw all the engraved labels for the last volume, several are given here which were issued only in photographs last year. It will be clearest for reference to state the number on plate xi., the reference to the photograph, and the comparison with duplicate labels already published.

Pl. xi.	Photographed.	Compare.
2	*Ab.* iv, 12	. . .
3	. . . .	*R. T.* i, xiii, 3
4	*R. T.* ii, viiA 3	,, xiv, 12
5	,, ,, 6	,, ,, 22
6	,, ,, 5	. . .
7	,, ,, 4	*R. T.* i, xv, 16
8	,, vii, 11	,, ,, 18
9	,, viii, 5	,, xvii, 26
10	,, ,, 1	*R. T.* ii, xii, 6
11	,, ,, 2	{ *R. T.* i, xvii, 29 { *R. T.* ii, xii, 6

The duplicate fragments are of the greatest value in any attempt to read these inscriptions, as the variants in arrangement show in what order the signs are to be taken, and what are connected groups. In fig. 11 here, the comparison of the reading with those named above, shows clearly that the *sen* sign of the royal name is to be taken in the sense of "breath," as in two cases it has the nose following it.

On plate xii. are various examples of incised marks on stone vases, which should be put on record. Those without references were found on fragments heaped together from various tombs in the French work. Fig. 1 is photographed in *R. T.* ii, pl. ii, 7. Fig. 15 is part of a *nebui* inscription. Fig. 18 is probably the *up ast* as in *R. T.* ii, pl. vA, 6, 22—24. Figs 20, 21, 22 seem to be all variants of one, and probably the same as *R. T.* i, vii, 11; from these examples the reading must be *mer-se-ka*.

10. On plate xiii. are some drawings of steles, which have not been published in photograph. Some of them are unusual, and need careful comparison with parallel names. On 151 there seems to be the name *Da-Khnum* "gift of Khnum," but with a very strange form of vase determinative, unlike any vases

known of this age. On 148 it seems as if the double hill *du* was used as a variant for the triangle gift *da*, and it should read *Hotep-du-Neit*, "Neit give peace." The painted inscription in red, 156, is uncommon. On 159 seems to be a hyaena. 168 is a fragment of a large royal stele, found in what is probably the tomb of Narmer; it is carved with relief in three different levels, indicated by different shading; the object appears to be part of a decorated façade (like that in *Deshasheh*, xxvi), and if so, the royal name was probably in the doorway below it, as on the inscription of king Ka. Unhappily no more was found; but, of course, there may be other fragments in Paris quite unknown. The gold bar of Aha, 171, is here outlined in side view, and the markings on the ends also shown; the photograph of the ends has been already published in *R. T.* ii, pl. iiiA 7, and described on p. 21.

11. On plates xiv., xv., the worked flints found in the royal tombs are arranged in their historical order. In the upper half of the series the flakes and scrapers are placed, and below these are the knives and fragments. The names of the kings are placed at the top of each column, and the letters of the tombs and some details are written on the photographs. In no other country or age has such an admirable series been found for the study of variations in the types and the rate of variation. And this only adds one more to the bitter regrets that this collection consists of only the scraps left behind after the shameless plundering of these tombs by speculators, with the full assent of the Egyptian authorities.

At the top the small pointed flakes begin with Mena, and disappear under Merneit; the flakes under Den are rougher, and such continue to Perabsen. On the other hand, the square-ended flakes begin under Den, but develop strongly and distinctively during the IInd Dynasty. The round-ended flakes are finely worked with wide flat sides; beginning under Zer, they are poorer under Den, and merge into the square-ended flakes by the end of the Ist Dynasty.

The flat scrapers are not of well-marked types at first; a tailed scraper is seen under Merneit, and a rounded triangular one under Azab. The triangle is sharper under Mersekha, and by the time of Khasekhemui the triangular scraper, long or equilateral, is the commonest form of flint.

The knives begin with the deep back curve, as in that found in the Mena-tomb at Naqada (DE MORGAN, *Rech.* ii, fig. 769). The handle by the first large knife does not belong to that specimen, but is only placed to carry on the figure. The curve becomes less gradually, until it is almost straight backed under Khasekhemui. The surface working, which is far below that of the prehistoric flints even at first, becomes rougher on the later knives, and the body is left much thicker and coarser. One instance of a recurved tip occurs under Zet. The small knives, with two nicks for tying them on to the girdle, are only found under Zer, see foot of plate. The sharp toe to the handle is most marked in the first half of the dynasty, and fades away after that until it is almost lost under Khasekhemui. The most typical series of these varieties for comparison is in the Ashmolean Museum, Oxford.

CHAPTER II.

THE TEMENOS OF OSIRIS.

12. As the excavations in the great Temenos of Osiris still need one or two years more of work to complete them, it is not desirable to prepare a tentative plan; but anyone wishing to follow closely what is described can use the plan made by Mr. Garstang, and published in *El Arabah*. Without a plan it is useless to trouble a reader with topographical descriptions, and hence the account here is restricted to explaining the relations of the various things found and figured in these plates.

So far as our excavations have yet gone, the history of the site may be briefly summed up thus. A temple of Osiris stood here upon the sandy edge of the desert, certainly in the VIth Dynasty, and presumably before the Ist Dynasty. Outside of the temple enclosure a town sprang up behind it on the desert before the Ist Dynasty, and mingled with that town are a few large tombs and some smaller burials of the Ist Dynasty. These seem to have been placed amid the deserted houses when that part of the town was unoccupied. This town spread for some hundreds of feet around the temple, and lasted on to the IVth—VIth Dynasties. Some time after the Old Kingdom a great enclosure wall was built, far outside of the temple ground, resting upon the town rubbish. A corner of this was boxed off with cross walls, and filled up with interments of the XIth—XVIIth Dynasties, known later as the Kom es Sultan, which was completely emptied out by Mariette's workmen. In the XIth Dynasty Antef V. rebuilt the temple with octagonal columns of limestone. In the XIIth Dynasty many monuments were added by Usertesen I. In the XIIIth Dynasty Sebekhotep III. built a black granite gateway.

In the XVIIIth Dynasty Tahutmes III. built a massive inner enclosing wall to the temple, over twenty feet thick, with a great red granite pylon on the back or desert side, opening into the larger walled area. Much of the larger wall had been destroyed, and a town spread over the space, as before in the Old Kingdom; but later, probably in the troubles of the XXth Dynasty, the old line of outer wall was built again, over the later town. In the XXVIth Dynasty the temple was rebuilt, and additions made in the XXXth Dynasty. Where the original shrine of Osiris stood is not yet known; but presumably it was the nucleus of the original temple, and therefore beneath the later temples. We have not yet cleared the temple site below the foundations of the XVIIIth Dynasty, and work there will be very difficult owing to the rise of the Nile level placing the lower parts under water.

13. The excavation of the temenos area was a difficult matter to arrange. On every side it was bounded so that no clear space could be begun upon; and I was obliged to start by throwing back along a line of existing ruins. In the higher part of the ground, nearer to the desert, the clean sand surface of the old desert was found beneath all the towns piled one over the other. But this clean sand was inaccessible beneath the water in every part of the temple ground bounded by the great wall of Tahutmes

III. That most important region we have only yet searched as far back as the XVIIIth Dynasty; but having now finished a large space outside of it, we can proceed next year to unload the temple ground on to the space already searched, and thus work down over it, leaving only the lowest levels to be cleared at the dry end of the season. In the whole space outside of the temple ground not a trace of any building of the early time was found except mud brick houses. We have, then, to deal with what was a series of towns, piled up in strata which are usually 6 inches to 1 foot thick.

To denote the positions of small objects found, I marked each with a trench number and a level. The trench numbers I have not published here, as it appears that there was a generally level spread of the town in all parts that we dug, for peculiar types of flints or pottery are found at closely the same level in different trenches. The levels were at first denoted in inches absolutely above a fixed datum point; but as work went on it proved more convenient and satisfactory to denote them in inches over the basal slope of clean sand. This sand gently sloped down from the desert to the cultivation, and hence absolute levels are not comparable, but heights over sand show the true depth of ruin. Every level stated on the drawings of flints, pottery, and other objects here is in inches over sand, or absolute depth of ruin at the point. Roughly speaking, the town began about the beginning of Dynasty 0, and the stratified material that was left untouched by the *sebakhin* rarely extended beyond the IInd Dynasty. The discussion of the relations of the pre-historic sequence dates, the kings' reigns, and the town levels will best be taken after describing the various material that we have found. In many places I dug through the basal sand for a foot or two, but always found it clean and undisturbed, and in no case did I observe any graves or hollows dug in it and filled up, though I

often looked for them carefully. The walls of the houses were sometimes visible for a couple of feet or so in height when a clean section was cut; but the bricks were quite indistinguishable, and the wall could only be detected as the interruption of lines of charcoal and potsherds by a vertical face of uniform earth. It was, therefore, not practicable to trace out the separate houses, or to make any plan of the buildings; and in no case did we find any length of uniform wall more than the side of a room or two, or any thicker mass than the usual chamber walls. There does not seem to have been any large enclosure or uniform mass of building, but only small houses. The whole compacted mass of wall-stumps, mud and sherds is so unified by pressure and wet — being saturated at high Nile — that only clean cut sections would show anything; and there was no discriminating cohesion in one part more than another.

14. Throughout the early town, flints more or less wrought were abundant. Thousands of flakes were found (of which a portion were levelled, and are figured on pls. xxiv, xxv): and some hundreds of worked-up flints, knives, scrapers, saws, &c., which were all levelled when found in undisturbed earth. The *sebakhin* had, however, dug over the whole site, and parts of it down even to the sand; and therefore many flints were found in their siftings which cannot now be levelled. Though some of these were fine examples, they are not figured here, as no exact historic value can be given to them. The drawings here were all made by outlining the flints on the paper, copying the edge flakes, and then drawing in the general flaking by freehand, observing the form of each flake carefully. Every flint has its level in inches over the basal sand, or the depth of ruin when it was dropped, marked below it.

Pls. xvi, xvii. FLINT KNIVES WITHOUT HANDLES.—On comparing these it did not seem that there was any restriction of types to special levels; hence these are arranged rather by the amount of curvature in the back, as this enables a comparison with any other specimen to be most readily made. The whole of the flaking is rough compared with the prehistoric work, and it resembles that of the knives of the Ist Dynasty tombs and the Hierakonpolis deposit. Many of the specimens are greatly changed in outline by wear; for instance, the snubbing of the edge of 27 shows plainly in the drawing. This snubbing is always on the side next the person when the flint is held in the right hand; and was doubtless the result of scraping away from the person. Sometimes a flint will be snubbed half the length on one face and half on the other face, having been held sometimes by one end, sometimes by the other. This wear may be noticed in the drawings of 5, 7, 14, 19, 27, 35, and 36, outer end. The wide finely re-curved knives 30, 35, 36, 37, 40, 41 and 42 belong to levels 22 to 65 (as the M tombs were cut into the ground, see below); and this corresponds to the first half of the Ist Dynasty, agreeing to the fine one of this type in the Naqada tomb of Mena's queen. No butt ends of this type of knife were found in the royal tombs, excepting perhaps one of Zet and one of Mersekha; but owing to only the broken pieces being known from those tombs, it is difficult to make comparisons. The tip 40 is much like one of Zer; and the recurved tip 39 is like one of Zet.

Pls. xviii, xix. FLINT KNIVES WITH HANDLES. —These seem to cover the same range of levels as those without handles. They are arranged here in order from the most concave backs to the most convex. The work is generally rougher than is seen on those from the royal tombs; a natural difference between working articles and royal specimens. None of the very pointed toes are found on the handles, and the blades are far thicker than the royal knives. We may well compare fig. 53 with the knives of Khasekhemui, the long narrow blade 60 with

the long blade of the same king, and fig. 54 is most like the knives of Azab and Mersekha. The last example, fig. 84, is of the XIth—XIIth Dynasty, as it is closely like those in *Dendereh*, xxii, *Kahun*, xvi, and *Illahun*, vii, xiii.

Pl. xx. THE FLINT HOES.—These form a well-marked group, none being found below 38, and most being within 20 inches, from 75 to 95. The form underwent very slight changes down to the XIIth Dynasty (*Illahun*, vii.). Most of these hoes show the high polish due to wear in use; and the mode of setting is seen in hieroglyphs of the Vth Dynasty, where three hoes in a line are bound on to the end of a long handle, at right angles to it.

Pls. xxi—xxiii. THE SCRAPERS.—These are roughly classed as tailed, irregular, and round; in each class they are arranged in the order of their levels.

The tailed scrapers are mostly poor and slight up to about 40 level; but from 36 to 51 there is a class of thick, carefully-flaked, pieces, with the edge often notched. After 51 only two slight ones are known. The history of this form is therefore very definite.

The irregular scrapers are mainly before 40; 22 being in the first 40 inches, and only 8 in the next such space.

The round scrapers are similarly distributed, three-quarters in the lowest part of the town. As in the royal tombs it is only when the finer-worked flints were given up that the rougher scrapers were buried, it is useless to compare the few scrapers found there with those from the town. At the base of the plate are two flint borers; a broken disc of flint, probably in course of working for a bracelet; and a flint core.

Pl. xxiv. LONG SCRAPERS.—These have all been used for scraping a wide surface; some may probably be misused knives (189, 193), but others are evidently made for scraping, as 194, 195, 198.

FLAKES are classified into plain flakes (199—

236), tipped flakes (237—266), worked flakes (267—281), rounded flakes (282—285), and square flakes (286—291). The simpler forms are pretty equally distributed; the rounded ends are wide before 60, and narrow after, much as in the tombs they are wide to Merneit, and narrow from Den onward. The regular square form does not here begin till 40, and we know that it continued in use till the end of the IIIrd Dynasty (*Medum*, xxix, 26).

Pl. xxvi. Three pieces of animal figures chipped in flint were found; and such are already known from elsewhere (see *Man*, 1902, art. 14). The figure 294 is certainly a crocodile, and the others may be intended for the same beast.

The smaller saw flints are probably all from sickles; they belong to the lower levels in the town.

The crescent flints are nearly all of the higher levels, over 50 inches. The use of them is suggested by finding a great quantity in a stratum of white sand and stone dust; this indicates that they were used like the vase grinders (pl. liii. 23—34), but probably for the earlier rough stages of drilling out alabaster vases.

The comb flints 315—327 are hitherto unknown; but it seems likely that they are a development of the round scraper, perhaps for scraping the scales from fish.

15. The stone vases, pl. xxvii, which were found in the temenos strata are mostly fragmentary. They show, however, the periods of several well-known types, which may all be placed here within the Ist Dynasty or a little before it. Referring to the stone vases which are dated by the Royal Tombs (*R. T.* ii, pls. xlvi—liii), we may compare here :—

Stone.	Level.	King.	Number.
Alab.	30	{ Mena	297
		Zer	298
Basalt	45	Zer	54

Stone.	Level.	King.	Number.
Alab.	27	Zer	491
Alab.	57	Zer	299
Alab.	50	Zet	156
Alab.	30	Merneit	330, 331
Alab.	85	Merneit	334
Alab.	64	Azab	306

It must always be remembered that stone vases are liable to be retained in use for two or three generations after being made, as we see by the secondary inscriptions on those from the royal tombs. But on the whole these agree, the town being mainly of the Ist Dynasty, and the exact levels we shall note again in section 20.

It should be observed that several forms here in the town, with pierced handles (levels 45, 23, 37, 58, 40, 28), are unknown in the royal tombs, and only once occur (M 16, 6, pl. xlv) in the large quantity of stone vases in the M tombs; they are like some late prehistoric forms, and seem to have been avoided for tomb furniture.

16. Pls. xxviii—xxxv. THE EARLY POTTERY.—The whole of the pottery found in the strata of the early town is here classed according to its forms, from the most open to the most closed. It might seem superfluous to give figures of so many slightly differing varieties; but it is just the minute variations which best enable us to study and discriminate the changes and different periods. Therefore wherever a difference could be distinctly seen, apart from the mere irregularities of form in each pot, it is here given for comparison. The forms are all numbered through, 1 to 211, so that only the numbers are quoted in the following account. Other publications of pottery are quoted as *N.* (*Naqada*), *D.* (*Diospolis*), *R. T.* i. (*Royal Tombs* i.), and M (plates xxxvi.—xlvii. here, of M tombs).

The forms 1—5, 8, 9, are roughly handmade, see *N.* R 1 and 21. These and the small saucers, 10—14, are so easily invented at any time that they are not important.

The everted bowls 15—27 are both of rough brown pottery (see *N. R* 24, 26, 28) or of polished red ware of poor and late quality (see *N. P* 15, 17, 18).

The brim bowls, 28—31, are of late origin, but of various ware; some red polished (*N. P* 14), some rough brown, but more usually of hard late ware (*N. L* 7, 8, 9, 10).

The inturned bowls are the commonest of all, and descend from early ages; they are divided into four columns here, the straight sided, the curved sided, the rounded sided, and the wide based.

It should be noted that the different classes of bowls were not in use similarly at all levels. The rough small saucers are all of 0 or 3 level; the everted bowls at 0 to 25, and one later; the wide bases usually 25 to 50; the brim bowls 19 to 85; the rounded bowls 18 to 115. This shows that fluctuations in fashion went on from one generation to another, within the wider range of the mere existences of such forms which cover much longer periods.

The rough-bottomed bowls, 57—62, were made by dropping a lump of mud into a hole in the ground, and then shaping it up by hand. They are all very thick, and of soft, poorly-baked mud; signs marked with the finger often occur on the inside of the bowls, and such are copied here. The earlier forms are flatter, the later ones more upright.

The great pans, 66—69, were probably used for storage, as also the ovate jars 70—77. These forms are not known in the graves, except very rarely a jar. But the great pans were used to invert over a contracted body, so as to constitute a grave; and they are commonly known to explorers by their modern name of *magur*. The pans are found in all levels, but the jars only range from 18 to 62.

The great jars with narrow mouths (78—83) were probably sunk in the ground and used to store grain. A recess around the mouth (see section in 81) was made to retain a lid. The levels stated here are taken a little below the top, at the probable ground level. The same form of mouth to a spheroidal jar was found along with a cylinder of Ka-Ra, probably Khaires who reigned either just before or after Khasekhemui in the IInd Dynasty (*El Kab*, ii, 2). This would be probably rather later than the examples here, which are at 68 to 88 levels.

The largest jar (Fig. 83) is much later, being found at 55 inches under the pavement of Amenhotep I; the height over sand is yet unknown.

The cylinder jars, 84—86, are of the usual late type, such as is found in the latest pre-historic graves, probably contemporary with such jars in the Mena and Zer tombs. The series of further degradation of this form is given in *R. T.* i, 119—129.

The minute forms, 88—91, seem to be models of the large jars 102, &c. They are all early.

The rough brown jars, 92—97, are of the form of the late ash jars of the prehistoric graves (*N. L* 30). In two or three houses long lines of these were found stacked against a wall; in one case 21 jars, along a chamber 145 by 86 inches, standing mouth down on the sand (fig. 92); elsewhere more than a dozen, mouth up (fig. 97); elsewhere a long line, mouth down (fig. 95); and in nearly all of these cases the bottoms were broken off.

The smooth, hard, light brown jars, 98—101, are not so common in the town as they are in graves.

The class of great jars, 102—105, is quite distinct from all others. The earliest is that from the tomb of King Ro (*R. T.* i, 2), which has the raised bands marked to imitate rope; this is a copy of a jar slung in cords, like the example carved in stone found by Amélineau (De Morgan, *Rech.* ii, fig. 823). For a small pottery model of the same see *R. T.* ii, pl. xxxviii, 1. Such jars were found by me with the remains of actual cordage upon them in the offerings to Merneit; and the impression of the ring of cord round the neck is usually found on the lower edge of the great sealings. The successive stages of degradation of these jars have been already noted in section 6. The elaborate pattern on 105 must be due to an archaistic imitation, or possibly the piece was dug out from the lowest level in early times; certainly it is not in place in the series at 63 level. The plain jars without bands (104) are of the same age as those with bands, see *R. T.* i, 1—12; but they are generally of a fuller form than the banded jars.

The hand-made pottery, with diagonal finger marks, 106—116, is well known in the Old Kingdom (*Medum*, xxxi, 15; *El Kab*, xii, 23); but it does not occur in prehistoric graves. It appears from the levels to belong to the IInd Dynasty and onward; and may be a degradation of the well-made jars of the Ist Dynasty, such as in *R. T.* i, 16—31, or the forms 122, 129—131, 136 here, which are earlier than the majority of these rough jars.

The jars with a deep collar, 118—121, are probably the latest stage of the ash-jar of the prehistoric graves (*N.* L 33, 34; *D.* L 34c).

The whole class of rotund jars, 123—140, are usually of hard fawn-coloured pottery, which is common in late prehistoric times. They run on into the IIIrd Dynasty, compare 129 and *Medum*, xxx, 11; and the Vth Dynasty, see 135 and *Deshasheh*, xxxiii, 20.

The little round-bottomed jars, 141—150, are rare in tombs, but common in the town: they do not occur in the lowest levels, before the Ist Dynasty, but are known in the prehistoric (*N.* R 63) from 50 s.D. to the end. The earlier ones are well shaped with a good brim, and they become ruder in later instances.

The small globular pots, 151—174, are common in the earlier levels, but are all more rounded at the bottom than the late prehistoric forms, *N.* R 64—69.

The model vases 182—187 are of hard fawn ware like their larger prototypes.

The ring stand 192 is one of the rudest forms. In 193 there is a combined cup and stand in one piece. 194 is a dish with lip. In 195—197 we see combined bowls and stands made in one. Such are found in late prehistoric time, 72—76 s.D., but seem to be quite unknown in the IIIrd Dynasty and onwards. The stand pierced with triangular holes (198) is almost exactly like one in *Dendereh*, xvi, 38. The large globular jar on a small stand (211) is an extreme instance of the combined form. The decoration of red lines on the fawn pottery in 205—211 belongs to the late prehistoric age. The triangular tube 203 is unknown elsewhere. Several solid cylinders of pottery (204) were found, with wiped lines around the ends, and diagonal finger marks; they were probably used to support a wooden floor above the earth, like the jars at Koptos.

17. Outside of the smaller enclosure, close around the Osiris temple, the town had sprung up before the Ist Dynasty; and when four or five feet of rubbish and ruins had accumulated, at about the earlier half of the Ist Dynasty, several large tombs (some as much as thirteen feet by six) were sunk within the town, just outside the temple gateway. Probably that part of the town site was unoccupied then, and after standing a couple of generations the houses had crumbled down, and the place seemed bare enough for a cemetery, although it was afterwards again covered by the town. These tombs were then subjected to such pressure and wet in the soil that their contents and walls are hardly to be distinguished from the town rubbish outside of them. It is only when a group of pottery or stone vases is found that we can be certain of the presence of a tomb, and it needs careful examination to settle the height of the walls. As will be seen in discussing the dates in section 20 the walls are traceable up to, or within a few inches, of the

level which corresponds to the age of the tomb; and hence the tombs were cut down through about four or five feet of town rubbish, generally to the clean sand (see top of pl. lxxx), and lined with a wall which rose to the ground surface of that age. The roofing was doubtless of branches, twigs, and earth—like the prehistoric tombs—which gave way, and let the rubbish from the surface fall over, and fill up the hollow. Most of these tombs seem never to have been disturbed; the bodies were unbroken, the jars complete, and the fine stone vases in place; but as no gold work was found, and the only valuables were some beads, and in one case copper tools, it may be that covetable objects had, perhaps, been taken away. One of these tombs was found by accident two years ago, and its contents are published in *R. T.* ii, pl. xxxiii, numbered M 1. This year eleven more tombs or interments of that age were found, and the plans are shown in pls. xlviii, xlix, the pottery in pls. xxxvi—xli, the stone vases in pls. xlii—xlvii; the copper tools in pl. l, the beads in pl. lii, and the flint knives in pl. xvii.

18. In the plans pls. xlviii, xlix, every jar is shown in outline to scale. The pottery is in plain outline, the stone vases are cross-shaded one way, the blocks of stone single-shaded one way, and the brick walls single-shaded the other way. The numbers on the vases are those which were marked on them during the clearing of the tomb, and agree to the numbers on pls. xxxvi—xlvii. The necessities of the excavation made it impossible to keep a regular order of the numbers, either in position or nature of the objects. Sometimes only a part of a tomb could be done at first; sometimes it was needful to remove all the valuable stone vases overnight, for fear of robbery, and do the pottery next day; sometimes a space had to be cleared to stand or kneel in, so as to reach the delicate parts of the clearance carefully. Almost every vase was

sketched into a plan as it appeared, with often some measurements to secure the position, and then a number was marked on it to identify it again. After making the drawings of the forms, the plans were fair-drawn from the dimensions on the plates of forms, fitting them all in to the dimensions measured as they stood in the tomb. The bodies were far too much rotted, with the wet and pressure, to be preserved; the skulls were kept, in some cases, on a lump of earth, but all too much crushed to be of any value for measurement: the positions were, however, noted carefully in all but one case, where it was broken up.

The direction of the tombs was parallel to the temenos wall in most cases, and they are drawn here with the reputed north upwards, really N.N.W.

The tombs are arranged here in the order of their character, placing next to one another those most comparable. This is not in the order of numbers nor the order of the age. They should be studied with the sections, given at the top of pl. lxxx, which show their relation to the native sand, and the relative breadth and height.

M 24, M 25, M 26 are three burials in clay coffins; they stood to each other in the respective positions here shown. The coffins 24 and 26 were of black clay or mud, 25 of white clay. For the figures of the vases see pls. xli, xlvii. From the stone vases it has been observed already that they are most like those of the age of Den, Mersekha, and Merneit, so far as we can tell by one or two examples. By being close together they probably belong to the same age, apparently that of Den; the town level of which time was about 70. Thus the levels of the coffins at 40 and 50 inches (pl. lxxx) would mean that the hole for burial was dug 20 to 30 inches deep. The position of these and all the other burials was contracted in the usual prehistoric manner; and in almost all cases the head was south and face west, the attitude of the prehistoric bodies. This is contrary to the attitude of head north, face either way, in which were found most of the servants of king Qa ; and face east, as the IIIrd Dynasty people of Medum.

M 17 is the only instance of a bricked grave containing a clay coffin. The coffin was at 50 inches over the sand (pl. lxxx) ; and as by the stone vases the burial can hardly be later than Merneit, when the surface level was 60, the black clay coffin can scarcely have been covered by the grave, but was hidden by heaping over the top. The body in the coffin was that of a woman ; that in the grave was a child, and at a rather lower level. By its hands was a small square packet of beads. The mass below vase 10 was a lump of soft white earth, like rough plaster, which was not found in any other grave. The vases are figured on pls. xxxix, xliv.

M 14 is the only instance of a burial with head to north. The length of the femur 17·8 ins. (452 mm.) is usual for a man, but extreme for a woman. For the vases see pls. xxxix, xliv. The base of the tomb was 11 inches over the sand, and therefore dug about four feet deep from the surface of that time. This burial was unusually rich in having seven flint bracelets on the left arm, besides one flint bracelet on the right arm ; also a flint knife (xvii. 28) under the head. In the earth over the body were black lines all in one plane, with streaks of bright haematite ; this stuff was probably a rush mat painted with ruddle. Between the bowl 52 and the wall was the skull of an animal (gazelle ?) By the head were about 8 inches of carnelian beads, about 6 inches of steatite tube beads, the same of green glaze ball beads, and some long glazed tube beads. In front of the body beneath the hand was a large rough stone. The thickness of the walls was measured (12 inches), but the height could not be traced. The south wall was not found.

M 15. From the bareness of this tomb, and the poorness of its contents (see pls. xxxix, xliv) it seems probable that it had been robbed anciently. The west wall was not traced.

M 18. This was another bare tomb with only the commonest pottery and broken stone vases. It lay next to M 15, and had probably been robbed. At the S.W. corner was the skeleton of a gazelle.

M 19. This was the richest tomb of all, having twenty-two stone vases. We see here, as also in the next two tombs, large blocks of natural rough rolled stones laid on the floor of the grave. These are placed at the head and the feet ; and in each grave they mark out the line of the cylinder jars placed by the head. It seems likely that these stones were the bases of wooden pillars or props which supported the roofing, and which delimited an inner space around the body. There may even have been a central boarded chamber with some objects placed in it and others grouped outside of it. This would be like the central wooden chamber of the royal tombs of Zer, Zet, and Den, with the offerings in spaces outside of it. In M 19 the stone vases by the head, and the pottery cylinders 9—12, would all be piled up within the chamber ; and the group of stone vases at the north end would lie outside. In M 12 the cylinder jars 14, 15, bowls 4 and slate, would be stood up inside the chamber, and the other offerings in lines outside. In M 16 the large slate 48 and alabaster 8 would be leaning against the chamber side, and the vases 6, 22, 37—40, 50, 51 stacked inside ; also the vases 10—12, 18, 32, 43, 45, 47, and the bowls 42, 44 leaning against the side. On the decay of the woodwork the vases would naturally fall over into the positions in which we find them. Thus the arrangement of the contents points to some inner framing of wood, which rested on the large stones as a footing. In the section (pl. lxxx) it is seen that neither the walls nor the interment reach down to the clean sand; within the walls is a layer of broken bricks and lumps of rubbish, and then curved strata of town rubbish,—charcoal and potsherds,—filling up the hollow, where the roof had collapsed. There is 7 to 12 inches of house rubbish beneath the walls; and in the middle mud wash up to 15 inches, and then broken brick to 25 inches over the sand.

A very curious point in this burial is that at 13 upon the knees was part of the knee bone of an ox, and at 14 upon the humerus was part of the shoulder blade of an ox. These bones must have been intended to act by sympathetic magic, in order to impart the strength of the ox to the limbs of the deceased. For the references to the vases see pls. xli, xlvii. The large vase 16 had the lesser one 26 placed in it, and 36 also in it beneath 26. Bowl 170 was placed in 70, and 178 in 78. The north wall of the tomb was not traced, nor was the thickness of the walls ascertained.

M. 12. This grave was opened up late one afternoon, and I planned and removed the stone vases before dark, but had to leave the rest for daylight; unfortunately one of the boys thought that I had finished the ground in the middle, and cleared it out next morning, so the attitude of the skeleton was not observed beyond the place of the head. Of course that was the last tomb that boy ever touched. The vase figures are given on pls. xxxvi, xlii, xliii; the P placed to some bowls denotes polished red pottery. On the N.E. stone was a slate palette 4d; on that the basalt bowl 4c, in that the blue volcanic stone bowl 4b, and in that the basalt bowl 4a. The alabaster saucer 8 was placed in two pottery saucers containing malachite chips; and the alabaster 9 was in a pile of six pottery saucers. The pan 38 contained wood ashes. The pot and saucer 43, 44 were high up on the west side.

M. 16. This tomb had walls preserved higher than any of the others, being 52 inches over sand; as the level of its age is 55 inches in the town strata, the wall is preserved up to the original surface. The body had a slate bracelet on the right fore-arm, and three shell bracelets on the left. Two heads, of goat or gazelle, lay before it; some leg-bones to the north of the heads; and behind the body many gazelle bones, and another head. The large pan, 20, behind the body was base upwards. For the forms of vases see pls. xl, xlv.

M. 13. This was the largest of the tombs, and contained the greatest amount of pottery, and also copper tools; but three other tombs contained more stone vases. So it is true of these tombs, as of others, that the pottery seems to replace the stone vases. The south part of the tomb was first uncovered, and cleared as far as beyond the feet of the skeleton, by undermining the side of the cutting. A marker was then put down beyond the feet, and the north part cleared while the south was refilled; the marker served thus to connect the measurements, but the whole space was not seen at one time, owing to the great depth of the earth. Over most of the floor a cobble paving of rough desert stones, about four to six inches across, was laid down. This paving did not extend up to the walls in most parts, but on the east side it ran out under the line of the wall, though I could not verify if there was really walling over it there. In the second clearance, of the north end, I did not observe any paving; but it was not easy to see, as it was covered with thick mud, and could only be felt for by slicing the soft mud with a knife. The section of the tomb is shown in pl. lxxx. The wall extends from 15 below the sand to 52 over it; mud wash rises to 12 over the sand, and above that are curved strata of town rubbish, and broken brick at the sides.

The body was peculiar in having the spine severed at the fifth vertebra, with five inches separation between the parts, and yet the arm lying on the severed vertebra with its bones in joint and quite undisturbed. It seems

C

impossible to suppose that the spine has merely fallen apart during decay. The right femur was 19·0 ins. (483 m.m.), the left femur 19·2 ins. (489 m.m.) long, which is a very full size for a male. There were four carnelian beads at intervals around the head. Behind the body were two heads of calves and the bones of a bird.

The vases are figured on pls. xxxvii, xxxviii, xliii. The large pottery cylinder jars made in imitation of alabaster were filled with clean sand. A bowl, 63, was inverted over 13. A second bowl was placed under bowl 12. In the deep bowl 2 was painted stuff (linen or leather), a bone netter, a rough pan, a rough brown jar, bird bones, and bits of limestone painted red. The saucer 4 contained white paint. The large jar 41 was in the earth outside of the tomb limits, and it hardly seems likely to belong to the tomb, but rather to be one of the jars left in the town ruin at an earlier date. Beyond the feet, near the north end, the copper tools were found lying together; the position is not certain, as they were moved in the course of clearing, and I had to rely on the workman's observation. With the copper tools described on p. 23 (pl. l) were also two polished black quartzose stones, doubtless used for hammering and burnishing metal. This tomb is kept at the Cairo Museum to be arranged as an example of the burial of the Ist Dynasty.

It is unfortunate that this series of fine graves was placed in so low a situation, where, by the rise of water level, they are now below high Nile level, and the soil is so wet that it can, with a little shaking, be poured out from the vases as a stream of mud. This wet has decayed all the bones, so that it was impossible to keep one whole, and it has also made it difficult to trace the walls or the structural details, or to find small objects in the soft mud. But having been buried over with some twenty feet of earth above them, these tombs have been preserved from later robbers, and we are able now to reconstruct in our museums these sumptuous burials of the earliest age of the Egyptian monarchy.

19. It is hardly needful to say much in detail about the pottery of the M. tombs, pls. xxxvi—xli, as the classes have been noticed in describing the pottery of the early town, section 16. In some plates it has not been thought needful to repeat the varieties of the large jars, but cross references are given from one to another. (Correct the lowest reference on pl. xxxvi. 45, from 57 to 67.) In some cases of large numbers of bowls no separate number was attached to each, but the stars put to some forms show how many examples were found. The large jars M. 13; 13, 14 are made of light drab pottery in imitation of alabaster. The bottle M. 13, 65 is of hard pale pottery, like all the late pre-historic bottles (*Naq.* L. 60—66). In the tomb M. 18 there were practically only two forms of pottery, the bowl 3 and the vase 4, and the slight varieties are not noted separately in place.

The stone vases, pls. xlii—xlvii, were found in all of the M. tombs; sometimes there were only a couple, but in M. 19 as many as twenty-two. They were almost always buried in perfect condition, for though the more tender ones have often been broken, the exact position of the fragments shows that they were buried entire. In one case, M. 18, the pieces lay as if the bowl and vase had been broken before burial; and as this tomb contained only very common pottery, some disused broken stone vases may have been put in, for economy. Certainly there is no sign of "killing" the vases of either stone or pottery at the burial. The alabaster cylinder jars are mostly rather coarse and carelessly made, as if for funeral purposes, and are not nearly as well finished as those of the royal tombs. The splendid tomb M. 19 is again exceptional in having much finer vases than the others.

It will be seen in *R. T.* ii, stone vases 77,

359, 360, 363, 364, that the earlier forms down to Zer are nearly equal in diameter from top to base; whereas the later forms swell out at one end or at both ends, as 374, 375, 377—392. This agrees to the M. tombs belonging to the earlier part of the Ist Dynasty, as most of the jars are cylindrical. It is remarkable that there seems to be a deliberate selection of all of the varieties of cylinder jar for each tomb. Some have no band, some a plain band, some a corded band. They are distributed thus:—

	None	Plain	Corded
M. 1	2	—	3
M. 12	1	1	4
M. 13	1	1	2
M. 14	1	1	—
M. 15	—	—	3
M. 16	1	1	1
M. 17	—	—	2
M. 19	2	4	4

This seems very unlikely to be mere accident, as vases belonging to one person, or made for one tomb, would probably follow one fashion. Different purposes seem to have been in view for the different styles of vase.

Most of the forms of the bowls can be identified with forms found in the royal tombs (*R. T.* ii, xlvi—liii.); but as this is part of the subject of the dates of the tombs it will be taken in the next section.

20. The relations of the ages of the various classes of remains is the main result that we gain from the past season's work. It will be clearest to deal with the relations in this order:—

    A. The dating of M. tombs relatively to the levels.

    B. The dating of M. tombs relatively to kings' tombs.

    C. The dating of levels relatively to kings' tombs.

    D. The dating of levels relatively to sequence dates.

    E. Joint relations of all classes together.

A. To date the M. tombs in relation to the levels we may make the following comparisons of the pottery with levelled forms:—

M. 1.	35	levelled at 42—50	ins.
	9	before 50	
	20	50	50
	8, &c.	49—60	
	33	54	

M. 12.	32	30—50	
	40	43, 48	
	15	49, 60	50
	45	50	
	47	54	

M. 13.	12	19 (?)	
	10	0—50	
	35	10—50	
	8	40	
	75	43, 48	45
	25	before 50	
	76	58 (?)	
	5	62	

M. 14.	29	54 (?)	
	13	after 55	
	next 4	42—65	60
	1	0—77	

| M. 15. | 17 | 40 | 50 |
| | over 17 | 54—60 | |

M. 16.	next 36	33 (?)	
	6	45	
	42 & 44	50	
	13, &c.	after 54	55
	5	after 55	
	37	56	

M. 19.	4	18	
	64	19 (?)	
	57	49, 60	
	69	after 50	60
	63	after 54	
	11	after 55	

The age of each tomb must, then, be taken as probably equal to that of various levels of the town between 45 and 60 inches over the sand; the value finally adopted for each being placed after the bracket.

The meaning of this in relation to the construction of the tomb must be noticed. The heights of the walls of the tombs (pl. lxxx) over the sand are thus :—

Tomb	Level of age	Top of wall
M. 12	50	45
M. 13	45	40
M. 16	55	52
M. 19	60	45

so that the walls where traceable extend to 3 to 15 inches below what was probably the ground level at the time; a conclusion which shows that our results by the types of the pottery are probably true to a few inches of level.

B. The dating of the M. tombs in relation to the royal tombs depends on both the pottery and the stone. Taking the pottery first we see

M. 1 ; 3   similar to Zer   ⎫
     51   about Zet   ⎬ Zer
     16—19   before Mersekha ⎭

M. 12 ; 45   Zer   ⎫
     11, 47   before Mersekha ⎬ Zer
     15   before Qa   ⎭

M. 13 ; 25—27   Zer   ⎫
     51—23   before Qa   ⎬ Zer

M. 14 ; 4, 6, 13, 17   all Merneit ⎫
     3   Mersekha ? ⎬ Merneit

M. 16 ; 21   Zer   ⎫
     27, 28   as M. 1, Zer   ⎬ Merneit
     3   Zet, Merneit   ⎪
     14—18   Qa   ⎭

M. 18 ; 4   Zer—Merneit   Zet

M. 19 ; 50, 75   Zer   ⎫
     57, 58   as M. 1, Zer   ⎪
     65   Zet   ⎪
     10   Zet, Merneit   ⎬ Zet
     11   Merneit   ⎪
     60   before Mersekha ⎪
     69, 94   Mersekha   ⎭

Turning to the stone vases we see that they may be compared with those in *R. T.* ii as follows; M. 1 being omitted as we have not the sections for comparison.

M. 12		M. 13		M. 14		M. 16		M. 17	
9 = 418, O		61 = 195, O		52 = 319, Z		50 = O		2 = 59, O	
8 65, O		250, O		40 62, Y		51 O		1 460, O	
3 165, O		64 59, O		107, T		45 218, O		1 405, Z	
3 250, O		62 98, O		54 423, T		46 168, W		1 52, Y	
13 434, O		———		———		42 318, Z		2 63, Q	
8 307, Z		O		Y		44 183, T		———	
2 217, Z						7 309, T		Y	
4a 244, T						49 66, Q			
4b 152, Q						———			
———						Y			
O						(50, 51 = Zer			
						R. T. ii,			
						xxxiv, 71.)			

M. 18	M. 19	M. 24	M. 25	M. 26
2 = 222, Z	31 = 65, O	6 = 265, T	1 = 150, U	5 = 456, Y
315, Y	15 267, O	1 446, T	———	———
———	6 304, Y	———	U	Y
Z	21 317, Y	T		
	17 304, Y			
	1 224, T			
	30 107, T			
	214, T			
	4 469, U			
	20 199, U			
	25 150, U			
	T			

Hence putting the tombs in their real order we see

	By pottery	By stone
M. 13 .	. Zer	Zer
12 .	. Zer	Zer
1 .	. Zer	—
18 .	. Zet	Zet
17 .	. —	Merneit
16 .	. Merneit	Merneit
14 .	. Merneit	Merneit
26 .	. —	Merneit
19 .	. Zet	Den
24 .	. —	Den
25 .	. —	Mersekha

The only discrepancy here is that 19 cannot be brought later than Merneit by the pottery, and Zet would be better; while it cannot be brought well before Merneit by the stone, and Den would be better. So Merneit should be best adopted.

We can now put the town levels thus equivalent to the kings' tombs as follows :—

Zer . . 45, 50, 50 inches level
Merneit · · 55, 60, 60   „   „

C. We can further compare the pottery of the kings' tombs directly with that found in the levels of the town. Not so many comparisons can be made as those by means of the M. tombs, but they cover a wider range of time.

Form	Level	King
35	0	= Narmer
84	12—25	Mena
102	50	Zer
86	55	Zet
150	50—80	Zet
176	25	Merneit ?
104	54	Mersekha ?
59	14	Mersekha ?
136	70—88	Qa
129	49—60	Qa ?
61-2	90—128	Qa
116	85—115	Perabsen

Some of these are discordant, but they are only those which were at first marked with a ? as being already dubious in themselves; the greater part are fairly accordant, and agree also with the equivalent levels ascertained through the M. tombs. To this we may add that a piece of the same quality of porphyry as that used by Mena, was found at 30. I should then conclude that the following list cannot be far out as a scale of levels equivalent to the reigns.

0 inches = Narmer or earlier
25   Mena (but see under D)
50   Zer
55   Zet
60   Merneit
65   Den

75 inches = Azab
80   Mersekha
90   Qa
110   Perabsen

D. Lastly we have the relation of the levels and reigns to the series of prehistoric sequence dates. Of course the end of the series is the weakest point, as there is no comparison with data that come after it, as in other parts. I shall here omit all comparisons with types that have a long range of sequence dates, or a range that extends up to 80, as they are of no use; also those ranges before 70, as it is certain that they cannot be in question here. The useful material then is :—

Type	S.D.	Level	Figure
D. 27	—75 = —7	—7	206
L. 40	—76*	0	131
R. 65d	—72	0	154
R. 34c	—73	0	45
L. 19b	—76*	0	52
R. 62	—77*	5	160
D. 27	—75	8	205
L. 30	—78*	5—22	93
R. 57a	—75	14 ?	184 ?
W. 80	79, 80*	12—55	84—86
L. 86	72, 76	23	197
L. 50b	78*	23	125
L. 78a	73	30	32
L. 17c	—79*	38	54
R. 1c	—72	40	1
L. 19a	—78	42	53
R. 38	—75	43	47
L. 44	—78	50	127
R. 34a	—79	40—60	36, 38

and by the series of cylinder jars

Type	S.D.
W. 71a	78—80 = Ka
80	79—80 = Ka
85	80 = Mena
90	80 = Zet, Merneit.

Now inasmuch as the knowledge of the range of sequence date of each type is likely to be incomplete, but not likely to be carried on too far, so it is truest to take the latest range of S.D. corresponding to each level. Looking over these I should conclude that the probable truth is shown by the starred instances above, which give in round numbers

S.D.	Level	King
76	0	
77	10	
78	20	Ka
79	40	Mena
80	55	Zet

Here it is certain that Ka = 78 S.D., and must come therefore to level 20; and therefore Mena must be put to a higher level than was done in the table of levels and reigns.

A final summary of the results from all the evidence together may now be given: remembering that the kings' tombs show the pottery of the *end* of each reign. The date is given in years merely to show the intervals, and not as implying any total accuracy.

S.D.	Level	King	Date B.C.
76	0	. . .	5000 ?
77	10	. . .	. . .
78	20	Ka	4900 ?—4870 ?
79	40	Mena	4777—4715
	50	Zer	4715—4658
80	55	Zet	4658—4627
	60	Merneit	4627—4604
	70	Den	4604—4584
	75	Azab	4584—4558
	80	Mersekha	4558—4540
	90	Qa	4540—4514
	110	Perabsen	4390—4373

Very precise accuracy is not to be expected from a scale of numbers of tombs, as the S.D. scale, or from a scale of rate of accumulation all over a town. But the general agreement is quite as near as we could expect; and we see that 5 or 10 inches is a matter of some perceptible value in the levels of the town site that we are dealing with here.

The close of the series of sequence dates, at 80, is best fixed by the cylinder jars which I have trusted, as they are generally in accord with the vaguer indications of the other pottery.

21. Plate l. THE SLATES, TOOLS, &c.—At the top of the plate is the expanded design which is painted on a bowl of rough red pottery, the outline of which is shown below. The painting is done with red ochre, coarsely put on with a brush. It was found at level 23, and is therefore about the time of king Ka. The animal to the left seems by the horns to be intended for the kudu, now known in Abyssinia; the design of birds on a tree is not known on any other Egyptian pottery. Beyond the two animals in the middle are probably two forms of snaring nets, and a goat and kid seem to have been on the part now lost. Above the drawing are some fragments of painted pottery of the late prehistoric style, with the levels where found.

A few slate palettes were found loose in the town ruins. They are all of late type, already known to belong to sequence dates almost as late as here found. Beside these see pl. xxxvi, M. 12, 4d; pl. xl M. 16, 47, 48; pl. liii, 12. A curious piece of yellow limestone from level 11 with four holes at the corners is shown at the beginning of the copper tools; one side is rounded and one flat. The use of it is unknown.

The copper tools were mostly found in grave M. 13; a square axe, a round-headed adze, a cutting-out tool (broken) and the ends of two knives; all these lay together at the N. end of the grave (see pl. xlix). Another square axe was found at level 53. These tools are of exactly the pattern of those found at Abadiyeh (see *Diospolis* vii) which were dated to S.D. 78. Here M. 13 is about S.D. 79, and the other axe about S.D. 80. The long double-edged cutting-out tool found at level 20 is wider than the form from the tomb of Zer (*R. T.* ii pl. vi, 24); for the series of such tools, and their use, see

Man 1901 art. 123. A small square-bodied chisel was found at 25 level.

At the base of the plate are some marks on pottery, others of which are on pl. xxix. They are of much the same nature as those already published, except the strongly alphabetic forms marked broadly with the finger O K and P.

22. THE AMULETS and small personal objects found in the town were not frequent; but they are of special value as being better dated than any found before. Pl. li, 1 is a cylinder of translucent Iceland spar, pierced to hang on a necklace, similar to the drop-shaped pendant of alabaster in tomb M. 14, see pl. xliv.

2 is a slate pendant which seems to be a model of a stone axe of a form not known in Egypt; found loose in top rubbish, so uncertain in age.

3 is a rather similar pendant of green glaze, also undated.

4, 5, are bull's head pendants of green serpentine, of a type well known in prehistoric time (see *Man* 1902, art. 14; *Diospolis* p. 26); and these prove that the form continued to the early kings though the origin of it was certainly forgotten when 5 was made, probably under Mena.

6 is a pendant of earthy green serpentine, perhaps derived from the form of a shell, such as continued in use to the XIIth Dynasty. Beginning of Dyn. 0.

7 is a pendant of clear green serpentine, shaped like the brilliant green beetles which are now brought to Egypt from the Sudan. Beginning of Dyn. 0.

8, 9, are two forehead pendants of thin slate and shell, of the kind usual in late prehistoric time.

10 is a piece of a model cylinder seal, made of clay, with the hieroglyphs *k m*.

11 is a cylinder of light green glaze, with three crocodiles incised. (Cairo Museum.)

12 is a cylinder of dark violet glaze, with incised hieroglyphs; these seem to read "give

the house of bread to thee"; the house of bread being an early equivalent of the *per-kheru* of later funeral inscriptions. This type of inscription is just that found on most of the early black cylinders, which mention offerings and provisions, and usually have a figure seated before a table of offerings; such cylinders seem to have been the earlier form of the prayer, which was later expressed on the innumerable funeral steles. Reign of Zer.

13 a fragment of slate palette from level 52; about reign of Zet.

14 a piece of carved ivory inlay, such as is found in the royal tombs of Merneit, Den, and Azab (*R. T.* ii, xxxix, 37; xl, 45—8; xlii, 71-2). The level of it, 40 inches, points to the beginning of the reign of Zer.

15 an ivory draughtsman, rather different from those of Mena and Zer, but more like that of Den (*R. T.* ii, xli, 74); this seems to be of the level of Zer.

16, the tip of an ivory arrow, of the form used by Zer (*R. T.* ii, xxxiv, 47), and the level shows the same reign.

17 a fragment of the incised black pottery with white inlay; from the level this may be about the IIIrd or IVth Dynasty.

18, 19 ivory pin with spiral end, and ivory cross-lined cylinder.

20 a shell notched as a scraper, probably for cleaning fish (see *Kahun*, viii, 10). Age of Mena.

21 a model knife of flint; age of Mena.

22 a model forked lance of flint; age of Den. This is a good link in the series of such objects; at first we find forked lances of flint in the prehistoric age, from the earliest times (*Diospolis* iv). Next there is a forked lance set in a gold handle as a funeral implement, of the later prehistoric age (*Annales du Service* ii, 131). Next there is the implement reduced to a model in the Ist Dynasty. After that there is this form in the sets of funeral offerings in the VIth Dynasty (*Dendereh* xxi) where a slab of limestone has the models of the various funereal implements let into it. And thus we reach the *pesh-ken* amulet, of which a fine example was found of the XIIth Dynasty (*Diospolis* xxv, Y 61, middle group), carved in carnelian, with a gold head in a wig as the handle of it. It seems also further that this amulet may be continued in what is usually classed as a double feather, on the mummies of the XXVIth Dynasty. Two forms of feather amulet certainly exist, the straight feathers, and the two plumes with rounded tops; a third form with pointed ends turned outward, is found on the same mummies with the other two, so it cannot be a variant of either of those; and as no such feathers are shown elsewhere this is probably the *pesh-ken* amulet modified by confusion with the double plumes. (See *Man*, 1902, art. 64.)

23 is one of the discs of pottery with ground edges, and a ground hole, several of which were found; this bears a sign cut upon it. Age of Zet.

The four sealings were found just outside of the temenos, in some Old Kingdom town rubbish beneath the portal of Ramessu II. They seem from their style to be of about the middle of the IInd Dynasty.

The fish-hook is about the age of Merneit. The bone netter or bodkin, and blue glazed button, are undated.

Pl. lii. The beads are all levelled and so approximately dated. The top string and circle of shells is of the beginning of the IInd Dynasty. The second string of Zer or Zet. The third string M. 14 is of Merneit; and the small beads, 91 level, must be at the end of the Ist or early IInd Dynasty. They are of forms well known in the later prehistoric age.

The limestone spindle whorls were abundant in the town. Many were undated, being found in the shifted rubbish. Those here of one date are put into the same column; and they range from the beginning of Dynasty 0 to about the time of Den. There is some change of form, the early ones being more regular and flatter than the later; about 30 a coarse cylinder form appears, and soon after larger and higher conical forms.

At the bottom of the plate are some later objects. The piece of a slate cubit has the digits 12, 13, and 14, marked on the top; on the edge are as many divisions as the number of the digit, a favourite way of giving a scale of all fractions of the digit; on the base are some fragments of hieroglyphs. The arrowhead is of bronze; it was found within the thickness of a brick wing of the Ramesside portal, according to the workman, and its appearance agreed with this statement; so this gives a date for the large quantity of such arrowheads picked up at Abydos. The piece of a large blue glazed *ankh* is of Ramessu II; it was probably a piece of temple furniture like the *ankh* of Tahutmes III (*Dendereh* xxiii, 7). The weight marked with four strokes is of black quartzose stone, 1590 grs. or 4×397. The lazuli bead was found in the temple with the XXVIth Dynasty sculptures; it bears the name " Psamthek mer Asar."

Pl. liii. 1. A fragment of crocodile bone appears to have been carefully shaped like a bull's head, probably as an amulet. Found loose, undated.

2. A flint flake has at one end an attachment which seems to be calcareous clay or cement: the material might be a natural concretion; but the symmetry of the form of it seems to show that it has been intentionally modelled like two horns. Unlevelled.

3. Disc of gold and strip with turned edge, found doubled up together; they fit so well that it seems likely they were stripped from a gold-headed stick. Level 91; beginning of IInd Dynasty.

4, 5. Pieces of glazed quartz, with holes for affixing. Found loose.

6. Limestone figure of a bird, found loose.

7, 8. Green glazed figures of baboons, found at about 70 level, age of Den.

9—12. Green glazed apes, and beads, tube and ball forms; slate palette with crossed corners. All these I removed from the earth at 28 level, and therefore before the Ist Dynasty. There are a large number of beads, and the whole seems to have belonged to a woman. The resemblance of these baboons to those of the main deposit at Hierakonpolis of the age of Narmer should be noted. (See *Hierakonpolis* i, xxii, 11, 12.)

13—18. Many pieces of pottery were found, which I guessed to be parts of fire places, and at last a whole fire ring was found entire with a deep bed of white wood-ashes within it. The forms 15 and 16 seem to come from an encircling serpent of pottery round the place, with its head turned inward to the fire; thus combining the agathodaemon—which was the domestic fetish of the prehistoric age—with the hearth place. The levels of the pieces are:— fig. 17 at 17 level, a plain zigzag like fig. 16 at 18 level; fig. 16 at 20 level; fig. 13 at 20 level; a piece of a corner with notched ledges like 17, at 28 level; and a piece like 14 at 55 level. Thus most of these are at 17—28 level or a few reigns before Mena; and one is of the age of Zet.

19—22. Many pieces of ribbed tiles covered with green or violet glaze were found, like those found at Hierakonpolis. The piece 19 is the earliest, found at 19 level, or some reigns before Mena; the others were from 42, 36 and 38 levels, or about the reign of Mena. The style of ribbed inlay ornament, and the coloured glaze on other objects, are both familiar in the royal tombs of the Ist Dynasty.

23—34. In many parts of the town stone grinders were found, which from their forms were evidently used in manufacturing the innumerable stone bowls of the early dynasties. The examples here are arranged to show the different views of the grinders; 24, 30, 31, 33, 34, are all in side view, showing the curvature which they would produce, 24 being for a deep cup and 34 for a wide shallow dish; the other grinders are placed in base view, showing the hollow or notch on each side by which they were held in a stick so as to be turned round. They were usually found in a layer of white sand and stone dust, evidently the refuse of the grinding powder which was used with them. The levels of these showed that they belong to all parts of the Ist Dynasty. With these we must connect the crescent flints (xxvi, 305—314), which were mostly found in a stratum of sand and stone dust, sloping between 80 and 50 level; from such association it is clear that they were used for the vase business, and as preliminary drills they would be effective on most of the stones that were worked. Their age runs throughout the Ist Dynasty. Similar crescent flints have been found in the IIIrd Dynasty at Beit Khallaf.

35, 36. These rough red pottery figures of a hippopotamus head, and a kneeling leg, were found loose in the rubbish, and therefore undated; they are of the same class as the early pottery figures from Koptos.

37. A very rough squatting figure in limestone, found at the base of the town.

38. A strange piece of a large object of red pottery, marked all over with deeply cut triangles; possibly part of an animal figure.

39. A torso of a human figure in rough pottery.

40. Pottery figures of kine, of which the upper one is fairly modelled: they were found at 55 level, about the age of Zet, in the S.E. corner of a space filled with sand, which may have been the foundation of a building. In that case the space was probably dug down as a hollow, and hence the town level would be higher then, about the end of the Ist Dynasty.

CHAPTER III.

THE OSIRIS TEMPLE.

23. As we have already stated, the Osiris temple occupied but a small part of the great temenos which was later built around the site. The temple of the XVIIIth Dynasty, which is the lowest level yet cleared on this site, had close around it a massive brick wall, some thirty feet thick; in the west side of which was a great pylon of red granite, opening into the rest of the larger temenos. As the plans are necessarily still so incomplete, they are not published this year; but a general surface view of the site is given in Mr. Garstang's *El Arabah*.

The temple buildings principally consist of two parts: the first, or easternmost, is a square building, of which nothing but foundations and loose blocks remain; the second part has still the lower few feet of the walls of two pillared halls and some chambers.

In the square building were blocks of the XVIIIth—XXXth Dynasties, and foundation deposits of the XVIIIth—XXVIth Dynasties. The halls behind were built by Amenhotep I, and perhaps added to until the XXVIth Dynasty. Outside of the whole temple block, in the south of the great temenos are other buildings of the XIXth and the XXXth Dynasty. Until the excavations are completed it is premature to discuss the exact history of the site. At least it may be said that as the town of the earliest dynasties lies just behind this temple site, it is probable that the earliest temple stood there also; for a later temple would not be built on town ruins, nor would it be likely to abandon the primitive sacred ground.

The inscriptions, as such, are dealt with by Mr. Weigall in chap. v; so here we are concerned more with the position and historical meaning of the various sculptures.

24. The remains before the XIIth Dynasty are not numerous (see pls. liv—lvii), as the work has not yet reached the true level of that age in the temple ground, and all the stones that have been obtained are re-used. The blocks of Merenra, Mehtiemsaf (pl. liv), were found in the foundation of the hall next to that of Amenhotep I: they are of slight and rough work, but show that some building was done in the VIth Dynasty, so more may be found in future. No buildings of this king were yet known, except his pyramid; so any further results will be of value.

The three pieces of large private steles, pl. liv, were found near together in the square temple site. From the work it seems likely that they belong to the VIth Dynasty. The left hand upper piece is from the left of a stele; the lower is the bottom of the right side of a stele; the right hand piece is from the upper right hand of a stele. These belong to two if not three steles; and unfortunately only one name is left, that of a mother, a royal favourite Adu.

The clay sealing of Shepses-kaf (pl. lv, 1), is the only such known in the IVth Dynasty; and other remains of him are extremely rare. The royal name is seen in the third column, and the first column gives his *ka* name, which was hitherto unknown. It reads *Shepses*, "the noble"; and it gives a further proof that the hawk name was that of the king's *ka*, for as this _ka_ name is _Shepses_, so the king's throne name is Shepses-kaf, "his ka is noble." This is the only instance of a personal name derived from the _ka_ name.

The Vth Dynasty is represented by the lower part of a limestone seated figure of Assa (pl. lv, 2). No figures of this king are hitherto known. The stone is a soft fawn-coloured limestone; and the upper part was originally joined on by tenons, the dowel holes of which are seen on the upper surface. The work is fine and detailed, making us regret the loss of the head and body. The inscription is merely the _ka_ name and throne name. The VIth Dynasty inscriptions have already been described.

The XIth Dynasty opens with an important stele of Nekht, a son of King Antef (pls. lv, 8, lvii). Unhappily only two quarters of it remain, which were found in the square temple ruins. The stone is a coarse, soft, limestone, which was cut very thick in order to give it sufficient strength. The signs are roughly cut, and were coloured red. The figures are those of a king Antef and his son Nekht, before whom probably stood a figure of Anher or of Osiris. The temple of Antef is named, which we might call the Antefeum in Abydos. And Nekht is the follower of the royal son of the _Heq_ Antef; so he must have been attached to an elder brother's retinue. The mention of the _Heq_ points to this king being the first of the Antefs, as the later kings use the usual royal titles.

Antef V built largely at Abydos, probably renewing the temple of Osiris, as he did that of Min at Koptos. We found many pieces of columns of fine white limestone (pls. lv, 3—5; lvi); and one architrave with cartouches reading in each direction from a central _ankh_, as on the slab of Usertesen (pl. lviii); but the edges had been trimmed off, so as to form a rough octagonal pillar in later times, and only a narrow middle strip of the face remains, so that

we left the block on the site. The pieces of columns do not fit together, excepting that lv, 4 and 5, may reasonably fit at an original joint in the stone. On pl. lvi the total height of the columns is indicated at the top by the first column, and continued below by the parallel inscription on the second. The dimensions of the capital are 18·1 inches wide at top, 17·1 below, 8·8 high; the shaft 17·4 wide at 24 down, but dressed narrow just below the capital to give it some projection. It is remarkable that, even in this temple of Osiris, the king is named as beloved of Anher of Theni. The piece of column on the left in pl. lvi is of rather a different style, and might be of a another reign, perhaps of Usertesen I. Most of these pieces of columns are taken for the Cairo Museum.

25. Of the XIIth and XIIIth Dynasty there are many striking remains; the colossal red granite statues of Usertesen I found by Mariette, showing that the temple was greatly adorned at this time. To the later part of the XIIth, or to the XIIIth Dynasty, must be attributed the head of a colossal statue of red granite (lv, 6, 7), which was found with other fragments beneath a mass of loose dust a little to the south of the Kom es Sultan in the great temenos.

The slab of Usertesen I, shown in pl. lv, 9, 10, and pl. lviii, is of a form as yet unknown. In the photograph (9) it is seen to be a thick slab, finished on the front and sides, but rough below with a projection downward along the back. It is about 9 inches thick, 3 ft. deep back, and 4 ft. wide. Now not far from it, also to the south of the Kom es Sultan, lay another block (10), of the same width, and of a depth backward which would just end clear of the projection in the upper block. What clenches their relation is that the two strange grooves in the front of the upper block (9) exactly fit over the two holes in the lower block (10). The lower block is quite rough and unfinished around the edges, and was certainly to be sunk in an unseen foundation. Hence the upper block must have been only a step, 9 inches high, on the floor. The holes seem to have been for poles to be set upright, in the line of the front of the step. On the flat upper face are three lines of inscription (pl. lviii), which from their style seem to be of the XIIIth Dynasty. Thus the surface of the step was always clear and bare. The middle line is rather more worn than the side lines; but the space between the poles, 13 inches, is not enough for passing, and the wear must be due to placing objects upon it. The whole arrangement is unlike anything that we know in temples elsewhere.

The ends of the large front inscription run round the sides of the block, bearing *ankh zet ta*; this proves that the step was not built into a line, but stood clear and apart, except at the back edge. The names of the king in the later inscriptions have all been carefully hammered out; but we can recover Ra-sekhem, and in the personal name three groups of different heights: the Horus name in three groups with *n*, is almost useless to us owing to so few examples being known of this period. Of the possible kings there are the Nos. 2, 15, 20, 74 and 88 of the XIIIth Dynasty in the Turin papyrus. No. 2 is barred by the Horus name *se-ankh-taui*. No. 88, Sebek-em-saf, will not fit the sizes of the three groups in the personal name. Nos. 15 and 20, Sebekhotep I and II, would fit well if written out s.b.k. | crocodile on shrine | hotep t.p.; but No. 74 whose name is unknown might fit equally well. The gods here honoured are Up-uat of the south, Up-uat of the north, and Osiris Khentamenti. This block and its base are taken for the Cairo Museum.

In the halls at the back of the square temple were several blocks of black syenite, from a large gateway of Ramessu II. On one of them is an inscription of Sebekhotep III, see pl. lix. It is shallow in the cutting, and almost effaced in parts by the crumbling of the stone, due to

salt. Behind the king was his *ka* emblem, a head on a pole, with the ka name behind it, and the description *suten ka ankh*, "living *ka* of the king" above it.

The fragment of a cartouche at the base of pl. lix is there completed as *Ra·sekhem·nefer·hotep;* an unknown name, but of the same type as *Ra·sekhem·nefer·khau*, Up-uat-em-saf. It might however be a combined cartouche of *Ra·kha·seshes·Nefer·hotep*, with a badly formed *seshes*, like *sekhem*.

The altar of offerings, outlined in small size at the left foot of the plate, was found in the cemetery G, lying still in place before a part of the front of a mastaba of about the VIIth Dynasty. The inscription is shown more fully above. The block with deeply cut inscription, next to it, was found near it, in the same cemetery. The two-column inscription of a *uartu* of the prince's table, and the seven columns of another such official, Sebekhotep and his wife Nefert-uben, were found last year in the XIIth Dynasty cemetery, D.

In pl. lx, No. 1 is a piece of a limestone stele from cemetery D, tomb 7B, found last year. No. 2 is inscribed on the front of a kneeling statue of soft limestone found in the temenos behind the temple enclosure, near the statue of Ptah-em-ua. No. 3 is a part of a stele of limestone from cemetery G, which bears the incongruous names of Ameny and Sit-pepy. No. 4 is a piece of limestone stele from the temenos, of the XIIIth Dynasty. No. 5 is a fragment of a sandstone figure of a scribe Ab. Beside these a large stele of limestone was found behind the temple, giving long family lists connected with the queen Auhet-abu; but as the copying of it occupied so long a time, it must be left over to appear next year.

26. Of the XVIIIth Dynasty the first important work was a large hall, about 30 feet wide and 40 feet long, the roof of which was borne by six pillars; three chambers adjoined this hall; and another and larger hall to the

north of it may be rather later in date. These halls lie behind the square mass of temple ruins. The walls yet remain about 30 inches high, bearing the ends of some lines of inscription around the doors; and in the hall and chambers were several loose blocks of sculpture.

From the sculptures (Frontispiece, and pls. lxii—lxiv) we see that these buildings were erected by Amenhotep I. His personal name has been erased from the cartouches, but his throne name is intact, which points to the erasure being done by Akhenaten. Beside Amenhotep there is a figure of Aahmes I (top pl. lxii); but only as deceased, since he wears the *menat* like Osiris, while Amenhotep I, then living, is without that ornament. Besides the above head of Aahmes, we may identify another at the top right hand of pl. lxiii; the features are like those of Aahmes, and it wears the *menat*. It has been back to back with a figure of Osiris, as on the upper scene of pl. lxii. All possible fits of these blocks were tried, and several were thus connected together. It appears that there was a list of offerings along the base of the wall, 28 inches high; then groups of the king offering to deities above that, about 42 high; and a second line of groups yet higher up, of the king and his *ka* about 36 high; or altogether about 9 feet height of sculpture, besides the plain footing to the wall. In the list of offerings possibly the left hand top piece might agree better with the base piece if transferred one column farther out, as the offering *henek nu* seems to end in *t nebt* at Deir el Bahri (*D. B.* pl. cxiii, lowest line); but if so a short piece must have been fitted in between the blocks in the upper part here.

These blocks were mostly fresh with colour when found; but, unhappily, an extraordinary torrent of rain which fell, washed away nearly all the surfaces, and destroyed the stones so much that several are now not worth transport. They had been all drawn, and the photographs taken, before this damage.

A great quantity of finely-sculptured blocks of Tahutmes III were found in the square mass of temple ruins. The largest was a long architrave with richly-coloured hieroglyphs, which may be removed to the Cairo Museum. This, and most of the rest, had been taken down by Aahmes II in the XXVIth Dynasty, and buried for the foundations of his temple. Many blocks that we have removed only bore usual figures, of Osiris, &c., and are not here published. One large lintel of Tahutmes III, which was still in bright condition of colouring, was sent direct to the Boston Museum; it measured 65 inches wide and 35 inches high. Another lintel, which was of the same width, was found broken up in several pieces, as shown on pls. lxi, 2; lxiv; it is of value historically, as it proves that Tahutmes II and Tahutmes III were reigning jointly together at one time, regardless of Hatshepsut, and each bearing the same titles.

At the base of pl. lxiv are two slabs from the square temple; that with the arm of a goddess may be later, but the sphinx is certainly of Tahutmes III by the work and portrait; the title over it is not known elsewhere. The greater part of a broken seated figure of Tahutmes III was also found, to the south of the Kom es Sultan. The slab on pl. lxi has part of the titles of Tahutmes III, delicately carved. Another slab bears the *ka* name of Amenhotep II, and names his *sed* festival, as on the pillar published by Prisse.

Within the square mass of ruins were found two foundation deposits of Tahutmes III in pits full of sand, showing that the site was not all dug out when the later temple was built. The deposit contained the usual pottery of that time (see *Koptos* pl. xiv), and copper models of knives, adzes, and axes (see pl. lxi, 5), with an alabaster vase inscribed, and a model shell of alabaster with traces of paint inscription. Some of the copper tools bear the name of the king, and probably all will be found to be inscribed when cleaned. The plan and position of the deposit will be given in the survey next year.

Another deposit pit was found, which only contained a green glazed plaque, broken up, with the name of Amenhotep III, and a solid stand of limestone of same king, pl. lxi, 3, 4.

The slab of inscription pl. lxi, 6, is injured by incrustations of lime, and has not yet been studied. The jasper head, fig. 7, is from some inlayed work; it is highly finished, and seems as if it might be of the XVIIIth Dynasty. The steatite head, fig. 8, may be later: but the blue glass fish, fig. 9, is of finely-cut glass; and, by the colour, not far from the time of Amenhotep III.

27. The XIXth Dynasty has left several sculptures, but not any large quantity of building like the previous age. The principal piece is a limestone statue of an official Ptah-em-ua, pls. lxv, 2—4; lxvii. He is represented nearly life size, standing, and holding a statue of Osiris before him. His offices were keeper of the cattle in the temple of Ramessu II, and royal scribe of the divine offerings of all the gods; and his full name was Amen-em-per-Ptah-em-ua, "Amen in the temple, Ptah in the barque." The statue was found over a deep square hole, not yet cleared out, at the back of the inner enclosure wall of the temple. With it was another figure in soft limestone of the great Un-nefer, or rather of his son Hora, kneeling and holding a standing statue of Osiris, pl. lxv, 8.

In the later hall behind the square temple was a squatting granite figure of the ubiquitous Un-nefer, see pl. lxv, 5—7. It was greatly crumbled by salt, and I was able to lift off the face in one block, the rest of the figure being too much broken up to be removed. On the back is the inscription naming his mother Maatinuy, or Maa-anuy, and his wife Thiy (see Lieblein, *Dict.* 895). While near the great temenos wall, apparently turned out from the Nectanebo temple, was a granite group of two figures (lxv, 9, 10), of Un-nefer and his wife Thiy, surnamed Nefertari. The splendid pair of seated figures in red granite, of Un-nefer and his father, with a long genealogy, found two years ago, is published in Messrs. MacIver and Mace's volume *El Amrah*.

Amid the varied ruins over the early town was found a stone building, of which the plan is given in pl. lxxx, "In Temenos." The native tale is that it was a great tomb, uncovered forty years ago by the *sebakhin*, who found three pounds weight of gold ornaments in it, which were taken by the Mudir. Our interest in it was that it had been built up from all kinds of odd stones that were lying about; and contained in its walls, and scattered from it, many inscribed blocks. Among these was the great stele of the family of queen Auhet-ab, mentioned before, and the pieces of a great stele of the high official Khay, with his wife Ymamu, pls. lxv, 11; and lxvi.

Among the minor pieces on pl. lxvi the trial piece with birds should be noticed; and the fragment of the *ka* name of Ramessu I, which is rare. The last piece in the top line is a rough flake of limestone, with the cartouche of Ramessu II scrawled in with a brush of ink. On pl. lxvii the inscription of Bay is on a piece of wooden furniture, probably not from a coffin, as he is not called *maakheru*. Two pieces of black granite squatting figures of Unnefer are copied here; one giving the title priest of Sokari, which he had inherited, see Lieb. *Dict.* 905. The two inscriptions of Mentu-em-hat, the great vizier of Taharqa, are roughly hammered upon natural blocks of limestone, which are lying loose in the floor of the valley leading to the royal tombs; one appears to record his visit, and the other, with *maakheru*, was probably placed in his memory.

28. The square mass of the temple of the XVIIIth Dynasty, was rebuilt by Aahmes II. He took down what remained of the previous work, and laid it in his foundations. He

enlarged the plan, but without caring to relay proper foundations; so his stone walls rest on the top of the brick retaining-walls of the foundation of Tahutmes III. On one foundation block are his cartouches roughly cut, at 528 inches from the inside of the S.W. corner.

The principal monument of his time was a great monolith shrine of red granite, in the usual style of such works, which are familiar to us at Esneh, Thmuis, Nebesheh, and other late temples. The flat sides of this shrine have long since been broken off and carried away, leaving only parts of the unmanageable top. The main piece has nearly half of two sides of the pyramidion, bearing a large cartouche of Haa-ab-ra in the middle of each side, flanked by the vulture of Nekheb and the uraeus of Uazit. The smaller piece of the opposite two sides shows evidently a similar design. The two pieces placed upright at each side of the plate belong to some other granite work; or possibly to the sides of the shrine, which may have been made during the joint reign of Haa-ab-ra and Aahmes. The form of the name, Aahmes son of Osiris, instead of Neit, is very unusual, and was evidently used in honour of this temple.

The upper table of offerings, pl. lxix, is a thin slab of limestone, roughly carved, with prayer to Osiris and Khentamenti for the seal bearer Heru, a son of Sit-Hathor. The lower table of offerings is a thick limestone block, with a deep tank in the lower half. It was dedicated by Aahmes II, with his usual titles; and was placed later in the temple of Nectanebo, south of the Osiris temple, whence it was cast out on the west side, in the destruction of the place.

On plate lxx are other objects of the XXVIth Dynasty. The bronze figures, 1—3, are part of a large quantity which were found scattered on the floor of the great hall, to the north of the hall of Amenhotep. Nearly all of these were the very common, small, roughly-cast figures of Osiris. Fig. 1 is an unusual figure of Horus, with the double feather of Amen. Fig. 2 is Sekhet; fig. 3 is the mummified Osiris.

Near these bronzes was found a portrait head in quartzite sandstone (figs. 4-5), larger than life-size. The style could hardly be referred to any foreign influence, except that of the Roman portrait school of the late Republic; and as that is entirely out of the question here, since nothing even of Ptolemaic times is found in the temple, we must attribute this solely to Egyptian sources. The modelling of the skull and facial bones is very good, and is of the same class as the fine heads in basalt which are already known as belonging to the XXVIth Dynasty.

The foundation deposits, figs. 6—9, were found in various positions. A square plaque of Haa-ab-ra, (fig. 6), had been placed on the top of the pit containing an undisturbed foundation deposit of Tahutmes III. A cartouche plaque (fig. 8), and a square one, were placed on the top of another such deposit. But the group of small objects, fig. 9, the alabaster, fig. 7, and a large number of plaques (figs. 6 and 8) were found scattered loose in the sand, near together, having apparently been the main deposit of the XXVIth Dynasty building, disturbed by the subsequent removal of the stones.

These deposits show the continuance of the style of the XIXth Dynasty, which was hitherto unknown at so late a date. The bulls' heads, haunches, grains of corn, and flowers, are all similar to the deposits of the Ramesseum, which we should not have expected after the different style known in the deposits of Ta-usert, Siptah, Psamtek I, and Aahmes. The materials are green glaze for the plaques, 6, 8; jasper, carnelian, green felspar, and glass for the small figures; and the same stones, with iron, copper, and silver, for the rectangular blocks. No gold was found. The meaning of the semi-circular slab of alabaster (fig. 7) is unknown;

but it occurs also in the deposits of Siptah, Psamtek I, &c.

To the south-west of the temple of Osiris, but within the great temenos, stood another temple, built apparently by Nectanebo II, as a fragment of a cartouche ending in *ka*, of very late style, was found here. The retaining-wall of the foundation is over thirteen feet deep. In the west end of the south side there were two circular-headed recesses, one over the other, 22 in. wide and deep: the lower recess at 58 to 102 in. above the floor, and the upper at 109 to 162 in. There were no deposits found in these recesses; the upper one had been plundered, the lower one was filled with laid bricks; but in the corner in front of the lower recess lay the limestone mortar, cake of resin, and little plaques of lazuli and carnelian, shown in fig. 11. In the south-east corner, just under a stone of the pavement, 40 in. below the top of the wall, were found similar objects, along with a square of copper, and a hemi-disc of alabaster.

The most unexpected result of the year's work has been the discovery of a high style of limestone sculpture under the reign of Nectanebo I, which preserves the traditions of the XVIIIth Dynasty almost unchanged, and shows no trace whatever of the surrounding influences of Greek art. In the square mass of temple ruin were found portions of four figures in hard white limestone, two seated, and two standing joined together. These were all more or less destroyed; but, among the large masses of chips, we recovered the greater part of the seated figure 12, and the upper half of one of the standing figures, 13, 14. The seated figure has the delicate curves, the fine proportions, and the restrained modelling, which we know best in such sculpture as the torsos of Nefert-ythi, and other work of the XVIIIth Dynasty. The standing figure attracts us by the masterly rendering of the face; for while preserving the classical Egyptian treatment, it has a full vitality and realism in the expression which might well have been copied from the best type of the modern Egyptian peasant girl. The present illustrations are only to give a preliminary idea of the workmanship; but the whole of the pieces are now in the Cairo Museum, and, when the figures are restored, a full publication of them on a large scale, will be essential. The date of this class of work is given by a dedication on the front of the pedestal of one of the seated figures, which bears the cartouches of Nekht-hor-heb, cut with the same refinement and delicacy as is shown in the sculpture.

D

CHAPTER IV.

THE CEMETERY G.

29. On the south side of the great valley which leads up to the Royal Tombs, a spur of the desert runs forward between the temenos of Osiris and the great temples of the XIXth Dynasty. The whole surface of this hill, for about half a mile back, is honeycombed with tombs. Those near the desert edge are so close together, and have been so completely wrecked by Mariette's plunderers, that we have not attempted to do anything among them. But opposite the old fort (the Shunet-ez-Zebib), and further back, only a few of the tombs had been opened in modern times. (See *R. T.* i, pl. iii.) During our first winter here, several of them were explored, and in the past season, we have opened up a good deal of the ground. The burials here belong to many different periods. Small interments of the prehistoric times are frequently found near the surface; and the pottery, and other objects, also occur mixed with the earth thrown up in constructing later tombs. A part of a mastaba of the VIIth Dynasty has been already mentioned, see the altar at base of pl. lix. Several tomb-pits of the XIth Dynasty have been opened; they are usually placed in pairs, one leading to the chamber, the other, about half of the depth, probably for offerings; deeper tombs of the XIIth Dynasty have also furnished us with the alabaster vases and beads of that age. In the XVIIIth Dynasty older tombs were re-used, for a burial of a child with vases, and a rich burial with a silver pilgrim bottle, gold ring, &c. In the XIXth Dynasty a great tomb was made here for a priestess Khnumy, from which we removed her granite sarcophagus lid, now in Cairo. But the principal use of this region was from the XXVIth Dynasty to the Ptolemaic age. One of the earliest of this group, containing five stone sarcophagi, was found beneath a large square pillared court of a few centuries later, G. 57 (see base of pl. lxxx). The next type of tomb was that with two arched chambers side by side, beneath a low mastaba of brickwork (see G. 50 pl. lxxx); these also contain stone sarcophagi, sometimes square, sometimes shaped like the body. Other less usual types of this age are seen in G. 68 and 58. Later than these forms are wide square courts of brickwork, which were filled up with two stone built chambers; these were evidently derived from the form of G. 50, but were later than that as the sarcophagi are debased. This form was modified to a court with pillars of brick, the whole faced with hewn stone, as the upper tomb G. 57; and, in another case, remains of a Greek pediment front of breccia, showed an ornamental doorway to have been an architectural feature. These great brick courts filled with stone work, have in all cases been quarried to pieces; and they are now usually full of broken mummies, dogs, and various organic rubbish thrown in when the cemetery was was cleaned up in later times. In the Ptolemaic times the tombs were crowded with bitumenized bodies; and soon the system of deep and large tombs gave way to that of small chambers, only just below the surface, containing only one or two sarcophagi in each. These sarcophagi are very neatly and boldly cut in soft limestone, with a plain wedge-shaped outside; and the inside hollowed out in curves, for the head and shoulders. After these, no later burials of the Roman or Arab age are found on this hill.

30. The prehistoric tombs always contained the bodies contracted, in the usual position, head south, face west; most of them were quite shallow circular pits, though there was one large tomb with over thirty pottery jars, mostly wavy-handled. All of these tombs belonged to the later part of the prehistoric age. The contents of the tombs of the XIth—XVIIIth Dynasties, not having yet been drawn, will be described when they are published next year. Fragments of a coffin, which seems to belong to the XVIIIth or XIXth Dynasty, were found in the chamber of a later tomb. The name Tahutmes (see pl. lxxi) is apparently unknown after the time of Ramessu II; though certainly the style of the writing here, might well show a rather later date. The first and second

drawings are from one side of a long strip; the third and fourth are from a similar strip, on the inner side of which is the fifth drawing; at the base of the plate are figured the two sides of a corner-post of the coffin. The style of these fragments is remarkably clear and delicate; the brown wood has had no prepared ground, but is left with the fine grain showing; the colours used are black for the inscriptions, green for the Nile gods, red and yellow for the other figures.

31. The large tomb containing five sarcophagi, found below the square court, marked G. 57 on pl. lxxx, is the earliest of the great tombs of the later age. The coffins, it will be seen, are lettered A—E; but E had never contained a burial, and we shall refer to the coffins here, by the letters A, B, C, D. The account will be clearer if I first state the genealogy; the letters prefixed to the names being those of the sarcophagi in which they are mentioned.

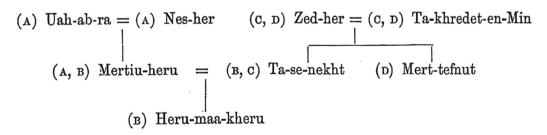

The variants of these names in different versions should be observed, as they throw a good deal of light on the true reading of such forms. For instance, in A and B, the eye of Horus varying with Mertiu-her; also the duplication of the letters *r u* and the plural strokes, for the simple termination of *heru*; the variants of Ta-se-nekht and Mehit-ta-se-nekht; also of Mert-tefnut and Nes-tefnut, which latter is probably an error for the similar form of *mer*. The value of the baboon reading *zed*, though rare, is already known.

On pl. lxxiii the name Ta-sen-meht, as copied by Mr. Weigall in a damaged passage, should

doubtless read Ta-se-nekht, as on B and C. On pl. lxxiv, No. 3 should read Heru-maakheru, and Nos. 4—7 should read Mert-tefnut.

We now proceed to describe the details of each of the burials, in order. Sarcophagus A is that of Mertiu-heru. At the head of it, marked 1, was the base of an Osiride statuette, and a model coffin with a jackal upon it, both turned upside down, see base of pl. lxxii; and at 3 was the canopic box figured on the same plate (lxxii). On raising the stone lid, a large wooden coffin was seen inside, inscribed across the breast and down to the feet, as copied on pl. lxxiii. On opening the coffin, the mummy was seen, covered with a cartonnage; on the head a gilt and blue headpiece, with ebony beard; on the neck a collar in bands with hawks' heads at the top corners; on the breast a figure of Nut with wings extended, coloured, and the four genii in gold on a blue ground, at the corners; down the legs a gilded strip, inscribed; and on the foot-piece a figure of Anubis. The whole of this, as well as the wooden coffin, was so much rotted that nothing could be preserved. Beneath the cartonnage, a network of beads in diagonal squares covered the mummy, 20 squares wide at the top, and 10 below. The colours were alternately five squares of green and one of blue, in stripes across the body. The left hand was clenched, the right hand open; the arms were crossed on the breast; and along the left humerus was a roll of papyrus, too much decayed to be opened.

The sarcophagus B is that of Heru-maa-kheru; at the head of which was placed the model coffin, pl. lxxiv, 3, a block base of an Osiride statuette, and a decayed canopic box. Upon the sarcophagus lay a mummified body, only 53 in. (1.346 m.) long: this was not quite adult, as the basilar suture was unclosed, and there was no trace of the third molars, but it seems too small to belong to a youth of normal stature. On the wooden coffin, inside the sarcophagus, was the inscription of Heru-maa-kheru, given in pl. lxxiii. The linen wrappings of the mummy were thick, and covered with pitch; the arms were crossed on the breast; the right hand was open, the left hand clenched on a bulbous root.

The sarcophagus C is that of Ta-se-nekht; at the foot of it was a model coffin (4 in plan), with a hawk placed on each corner, and a jackal on the top; while between B and C was another model coffin, with figures of genii holding knives, painted on its sides. Portions of a wooden canopic box were also found, bearing the inscription given in pl. lxxiii

(named there Ta-sen-meht). Inside the stone coffin was a wooden coffin, with an inscription in which the name is always spelt Tay-nekht, see pl. lxxiii. Upon the mummy was a diagonal network of beads, in vertical stripes of black and green alternately, with yellow ball-beads at the junctions.

The sarcophagus D is that of Mert-tefnut. By the foot of it was a block base of an Osiride statuette (7 in the plan); and on the other side of the tomb, next to B, was the white painted canopic box figured in pl. lxxiv, 4—7, (3 in plan). The wooden coffin inside bore an inscription, the only legible part of which is given in pl. lxxiii. On the mummy was a diagonal network of beads, in horizontal rows of five green squares and one blue square alternately. Around these sarcophagi were many other fragments of funeral furniture, like those already described; but so completely eaten by white ants that they could not be examined or preserved.

The sarcophagus E had its stone lid propped up with a course of bricks; this was evidently done in order to open it easily for the next burial, but it was found empty and unused.

32. An important class of tombs at Abydos are the large subterranean vaults, with a superstructure above them. These were restored by Mariette as brick pyramids with a central domed chamber; and his restoration has passed into a familiar item in later books. He also attributed these to the XVIIIth Dynasty. But apparently both this restoration and this date are wrong.

A typical tomb of this class is shown in plan and section on pl. lxxx, G. 50 : and a view of the superstructure is on pl. lxxix, 10. In the first place, was this sloping outside ever carried up to a point, as a pyramid? If it had been of such a form, an immense mass of broken brickwork would have resulted from the collapse of the pyramid. Yet in no case was any fallen mass of bricks found by us within the outer wall;

and the space between the wall sides was always lower than the walls themselves, which could not be the case if a mass of bricks, some thirty or forty feet high, had been disintegrated above the tomb. Further, in the instance G. 50 a great mass of gravel, which had been dug out when constructing the chambers, was thrown back over the tomb. This gravel had covered over the surrounding wall and perfectly preserved it: and it could thus be seen that the wall was finished off quite level all round; and though sloping smoothly outside, it was left rough on the inside. The only possible conclusion from the facts is that the surrounding wall was that of a mastaba above the tomb, to retain a mass of gravel covering the tomb; exactly as, long before, over the tomb of king Zet. The whole restoration of these tombs as pyramids then is impossible.

The age of the burials in these tombs, in every one that we excavated, was of about the XXXth Dynasty; hence the attribution of them to the earlier ages is impossible.

The photograph, lxxix, 10, is taken looking along one side of the sloping mastaba, the measuring rod set up at the side being vertical. The straight inside of the lower part of the wall, is replaced at the corner by overhanging courses, each projecting beyond the course below, until the square base is replaced inside by a circular top. The purpose of this was to strengthen the wall at the corners, so that the pressure of the gravel filling should not bulge it open.

The construction of some other tombs may be also noted. The great arched tomb G. 68 (pl. lxxx) is unique, so far as I have seen. Only one chamber was observed; but the mass is square at the top, obviously to contain a second chamber. The ancient plunderers had not tried to reach the doorway, but had sunk a shaft down through the outer wall from the top, and so revealed the successive courses of arching. The tomb only contained an accumulation of broken mummies, thrown in from other tombs.

The small tomb G. 61 was very different to any other. Between two vaulted chambers, near the surface, a stone sarcophagus had been placed; and brick recesses A, B, built at the sides, to hold the funeral furniture.

The fine tomb G. 58 contains the largest chamber that we found. A wide well-pit leads through a doorway to an arched chamber; and descending the steps in that, another doorway leads into a grand vaulted chamber over twenty feet long, nine feet wide, and fourteen and a half feet high. A slope of brickwork led down to the sarcophagus at the bottom.

33. We now turn to the contents of the tombs of the XXXth Dynasty. The tomb of Zedher, G. 50, was the most important, as being extensive and undisturbed. The west chamber was filled with clean sand up to the spring of the arch, perhaps to prevent the crushing of the wall; as, when the sand was removed, the arch crushed down and collapsed. This sand entirely covered the figure-shaped sarcophagi in this chamber. The sarcophagus A contained only a plain mummy without ornament or amulets.

The sarcophagus B was the most important, containing the mummy of Zedher. There was no inner wooden coffin, but only a wooden tray beneath the body. Upon the breast, outside of the wrappings, lay a set of glazed pottery amulets, the plan of which was noted by my wife, as shown on the left at the base of pl. lxxviii. The order was evidently confused by some parts of the strings of figures having been turned over in laying them down; and they may be pretty safely restored to the order shown on the right hand. Within the wrappings there was another set of amulets, made of various stones, the actual positions of which I very fully noted, as on the left at top of pl. lxxviii; here again some of the rows or strings had been twisted over in placing them, so that the original order was probably as on the right. The materials are limestone (l), haematite (h), steatite (s), beryl (b), obsidian (o), faience (f), black limestone (b.l.), lazuli (z), brown limestone (br. l.), porphyry (p), red glass (g), and carnelian (c). A few ball beads lay among these, the intended place of which could not be fixed. Beneath the head was the bronze hypocephalus, pl. lxxvi, and fig. 5 on pl. lxxix, which has no personal name; the example with the name Zedher, born of the lady Uza au (? Uza Heru), pl. lxxvii, G. 50 c, and pl. lxxix, 3, was found in sarcophagus C. Outside of the sarcophagus at the head were two boxes of ushabtis, shown in the plan. One box contained 198, the other 196 figures; examples of these are the 1st, 3rd and 5th in fig. 1 pl. lxxix. Beneath the western box was a great quantity of much ruder ushabtis, such as the 2nd and 4th of the above group. The better ushabtis were of fairly hard, dark, greeny-blue glaze, inscribed in ink. The mixture of two such different qualities of figures at one time, shows that there was much variety of manufacture. The numbers recall those of Horuza at Hawara, 203 and 196; evidently 200 figures was the regulation number for each of the pair of deposits.

The sarcophagus C contained a coarse wooden coffin of figure form, with gilt face. Within that was an inner wooden coffin, with a square plinth; an engraved inscription in columns down the front was entirely eaten away by white ants; it had a blue striped wig, and inlaid eyes of glass; and on the breast was a roll of the Book of the Dead much rotted. The mummy inside had gilt cartonnage for the face, pectoral, collar, winged figure of Nut, and strip of inscription and 12 cross-bands on the legs. All of this was too much rotted to be moved. Beneath the head was the largest bronze hypocephalus, pl. lxxvii, G. 50 c, and lxxix, 3, with the name of Zedher. One splint bone of the mummy had been broken during life.

The sarcophagus D, of Nebta-ahyt, wife of Zedher, contained an outer wooden case, with inscriptions down the front on stucco, all destroyed by white ants. At the left side of it an Osiride wooden figure, gilt, and inscribed; containing a bundle of fibres of papyrus (apparently a cheap substitute for a document) wrapped in cloth. The inner coffin of wood had the wig painted blue, and the eyes inlaid with glass, which was entirely rotted and brittle; the coffin was eaten by white ants. On the mummy was a cartonnage decoration, gilded; on the face a head piece; on the breast the deep collar, a pectoral, and the figure of Nut with outspread wings; below that a bier, and the four genii; and on the legs a strip of inscription naming "the Osirian Neb-ta-ahyt, *maa-kheru;* daughter of the prophet, the royal scribe Nefer-ra-ab, *maa-kheru;* born of Ta-du-mehit (?)." This gilt cartonnage had no support from the cloth, with which it had been backed, as that had entirely gone to powder; it merely consisted of thin gold leaf, and a film of stucco. The gold leaf gave some slight tenacity to it; and by carefully shifting a portion at a time on to a slip of card, it was lifted off the mummy. Then it was transferred to a sheet of card covered with paraffin wax, and melted into the wax with a hot iron. In this way nearly the whole is now preserved unalterable, and as strong as new work. Beneath the head of the mummy was the small hypocephalus, lxxvii, G. 50 D, and lxxix, 4; and on this was a pile of small amulets of stone, like those of Zedher, but of poorer work.

We now turn to the west chamber. This was evenly filled with sand, entirely covering the stone figure-shaped sarcophagi. Lying upon the sand in the axis of the chamber, above the sarcophagi, were two painted canopic boxes, 13 inches square, 22 inches high. The lids lay loose, with a hawk figure on the top, painted, with gilt face. In one box were mummified viscera in wrappings. By the body was a mummified hawk in wrappings, but headless; also an Osiride figure, on a block base 20 × 7 inches, painted on top and sides. A clean vertebra, a finger bone, and two bits of a tibia, lay loose on the sand by the funereal furniture. Throughout the sand filling many ushabtis were found lying apart, of which examples are given on pl. lxxix, 2. These are brightly glazed, of a brilliant light blue; some with purple wigs; and others larger, with purple wigs and inlaid purple inscription for the priest of Hathor and Uazit, Peduasar son of Zedher. It is thus well settled that this style, which is well known in late times, immediately followed on the very degraded style found in ushabtis of Zedher. The ushabtis were mixed throughout the sand around the three burials; three were in the sand within the sarcophagus G, the lid of which was tilted; but more than half lay in one group north of that. The total numbers were, plain 266, purple heads 83, inscribed 36; the total of 385 seems to have been originally 400, like the deposits already noticed.

The sarcophagus E was that of Horuza, son of Zedher and Nebta-ahyt. The figure-shaped lid is shewn in pl. lxxix, 7; the inscription in pl. lxxv. [The lithograph should be corrected; col. i, 4 up, *neb per* without a blur; col. iii, 5 up, no blur between *ma a;* col. iv, 7 up, add *t* before *a*.] There was no inner coffin; and the cartonnage on the body was coloured, and not gilt except on the face. On the breast was the deep collar, the scarab and wings, the winged Nut, the bier with Isis, Nebhat, and four genii, the leg cover with red and white bands and garland pattern, all of it too much rotted to be moved. On the neck were three heart amulets and an *uza* eye; on the body a red jasper girdle tie, a two-finger amulet, and a large heart scarab on the right side in the body.

The sarcophagus F was that of Pedu-en-ast, son of Zedher and Nebta-ahyt. The lid is painted with red hieroglyphics in outline, given here in pl. lxxv. The style of the head is coarse and poor. The body was covered with cartonnage, like that of Horuza.

The sarcophagus G was that of Peduasar, as the ushabtis were for him, and there is no other unnamed burial in the tomb. But the sarcophagus, though of the fine style of that of Horuza, was left quite plain. The lid was tilted over 20° toward F: the inside was partly filled with sand, and three of the ushabtis lay upon the sand. At the neck of the mummy was a bunch of amulets; some threaded in order, as a *uaz* sceptre, 4 hearts, scarab, double feather, 2 eyes, frog, eye, scarab, eye, Horus seated, and *sam*; some also loose, as scarabs, double feather, *aper*, heart, eyes, and girdle tie. A large heart scarab lay in the pelvis.

All of these sarcophagi are taken to the Cairo Museum.

34. The other large tombs need but little notice, as nothing was found intact in them. The tomb of Hapi-men was different to any other (see pl. lxxx, G. 61), as the sarcophagus was put in between two other tomb chambers, and had two brick hollows, A, B, at the sides of it for the funereal furniture. In A was a box of ushabtis, poorer than those of Pedu-asar, and evidently later examples of the same family; 30 were plain small figures, 2 were larger, and one was inscribed in a line down the front, for Hap-men. Over the ushabti box were two Osiride figures and a hawk of wood. In B was a canopic box, very carefully painted with much detail, containing two long round packets of salt; and a figure of Nebhat. All of this woodwork was destroyed by white ants. Within the square stone sarcophagus was an inner stone sarcophagus of the figure form. The face was of rather debased work, but carefully coloured in the eyes; and down the front was a collar, engraved and painted, and a line of inscription, see pl. lxxv. Both of the sarcophagi had been broken through at the side; and the mummy was torn to pieces over the breast, by ancient

plunderers in search of amulets. Torn from the breast was the pectoral, and on the feet was the foot case, shown in pl. lxxix, 9. These are well made and finely painted. Below the mummy, about the middle, was the bead fringe, figure 8; probably displaced from the neck. And at the side of the feet was a small mummified dog (?), carefully swathed in wrappings.

The great tomb G 58, pl. lxxx, had been utterly plundered, and partly filled with broken coffins and rubbish. The original sarcophagus was found in place, and most of the pieces of the lid. It was figure-shaped, larger than any other such sarcophagi, and of a fine hard crystalline limestone. The inscription, as far as it could be recovered, gives the name of Nefert-iut, a chantress of Khent amentit, and is copied in pl. lxxxv. Two fragments which cannot be put in place, are shown at the side.

In the great court G. 57 a lid of a sarcophagus was found, broken in two, and bearing an inscription in red paint. This is photographed on pl. lxxix, 6, and has been copied in facsimile but is not yet published.

Later than all these a tomb of the type of G. 50 had been stripped of its chambers; and on the floor of the open court which was left, rows of mummies were laid, side by side. On some of these were networks of blue tube beads, of the poorest kind; and the scarab and wings, and four genii, of dark blue rough glaze. By these were pieces of box coffins, made of wood painted red, with green inscriptions, rude and poor; and the latest canopic boxes of rough wood, either left plain, or with very coarse figures of the genii painted in red. These boxes instead of containing the mummified viscera only had linen packets of broken potsherds in them. On the floor amid the mummies were hundreds of brown pottery ushabtis, very roughly made, and coloured red, black, or blue. These seem to be the very latest stage of the style of burial which began in the XXVIth Dynasty.

CHAPTER V.

THE INSCRIPTIONS.

By A. E. Weigall.

35. The inscriptions discovered this year at Abydos are very varied in their nature and date, and represent many of the important periods from the VIth to the XXXth Dynasty. The majority were found in the Temple of Osiris, but the late sarcophagi and funeral furniture were taken from the Ptolemaic cemetery, known as "G," to the south-west of the Osiris enclosure. Although not of extreme importance, these inscriptions add a number of new names to the aristocracy of Ancient Egypt, and repeat with no little interest those of many of its kings. That this material has been placed in the hands of the present writer is due to the kindness of Prof. Petrie; and help has been most generously given in the clearing up of some difficult points by Mr. Percy Newberry, Mr. Herbert Thompson, and Mr. Alan Gardiner. Especial thanks must be rendered to Mr. Thompson for permitting free use to be made of his notes upon the subject of the hypocephali.

Pl. liv, 1. Three fragments of limestone false doors belonging to a Prince (or Princes) of Abydos whose name is unfortunately lost. His titles are *erpá ḥá* Hereditary Prince, *smer uáti* Chiefly Companion, *kheri ḥeb* Lector, *ḥeri dep aá ne Ábdu* Prince of Abydos, *mer neter per* Superintendent of the Temple. He is also connected with the *per net Ánḥer* Temple of Anhur. His mother was the *seten kheker* Royal Handmaid, Ad. The inscription speaks of him in the usual laudatory terms, among which we may notice that he was *ur em áaut-f* great in his office, *ser em sáh-f* lordly in his nobility,

ser em hát . . . . chief among the princes . . ., and *ur em Pe áau em Dep* great in Pe, venerable in Dep—these being the two sacred shrines of the city of Buto (Brugsch, *Aegypt*, p. 239). Osiris Temple. Dyn. VI.

2. Upon this plate will also be noticed two limestone fragments, inscribed with the cartouche of Mereura. In the first he is called . . . . *seten báti Mer-ne-Rá de ánkh ded usr ánkh zetta* 'The King of Upper and Lower Egypt, Merenra, endowed with life, stability, and power, living for ever'; and in the second he holds the usual title 'The double Horus of Gold.' Osiris Temple. Dynasty VI.

Pl. lvi. Portions of some hexagonal limestone columns, placed in position in the plate in order to show the original style of construction. The largest fragment reads . . . . *seten báti Rá-nub-kheper se Rá Ántef Anḥer neb Theni meri de ánkh ded ust* . . . . 'The King of Upper and Lower Egypt, Ra-nub-kheper, son of the Sun, Antef [the Fifth,] beloved of Anhur Lord of Theni, endowed with life, stability, and power . . . .' The other fragments give the usual formulae, such as *se Rá ne khat-f mer-f* 'Son of the Sun, the beloved of his body'; and *de ánkh ded usr neb senb neb má Rá* 'endowed with all life, stability, power, and all health, sun-like . . . . .' Osiris Temple. Dyn. XI.

Pl. lvii. Two fragments of a limestone stele of Prince Nekht, the son of Antef the Fifth. It is of rough workmanship, and there are many obvious errors in the hieroglyphs. In the upper portion we have the figure of the

owner, who is called *seten se ḥeri pezetu Nekht*
'The Royal Son, Commander of the Archers,
Nekht,' and of his father, the *neter nefer* 'good
god,' i.e. the King. The first line of the
horizontal inscription repeats the titles of Nekht;
and an interesting point to be observed here
occurs in the fragment of the first portion,
where the title *seten se ne ḥeq Ȧn[tef]* 'The
royal son of the *ḥeq*-prince Antef' appears.
The second line speaks of the *ḥet Ȧntef em
Ȧbdu* 'Temple of Antef in Abydos,' some
remains of which were excavated this year;
and the third repeats the titles. Then follows
an inscription in five lines of a religious character; and in the ninth line the titles again
appear, followed by an invocation to the
[priests,] *uȧb*-priests, children, and lectors, that
they may pray for funeral offerings, all good
and pure things, an entrance into the underworld, and a coming forth by day, for the
deceased. Osiris Temple. Dyn. XI.

36. Pl. lviii. A large limestone lintel [?]
inscribed with the cartouches *Rȧ-kheper-ka* and
Sen-usrt, i.e. Usertesen I. Along the face of
the stone are three faint lines of a later—
probably XIIIth Dynasty—inscription, the
cartouche in each case being erased. The first
reads *ȧnkh neter nefer neb ȧri khet se Rȧ . . . . . .
Up-uaut res meri de ȧnkh ded usr mȧ Rȧ zetta.*
'The living One, the Good God, Creator of
Things, Son of the Sun, ..., beloved of
Anubis of the South, endowed with life,
stability, and power, Sun-like for ever.' The
second reads *ȧnkh Her . . . . Rȧ . . . . . .
khent Ȧmentet meri de . . . . .* 'The living
Horus, ..., Ra . . . . . ., beloved of
[Osiris] Khent-Amenti, endowed [with life,
stability, etc.';] and the third *ȧnkh neter
nefer neb taui Rȧ . . . . . Up-uaut meh meri
de ȧnkh* etc. 'The Living One, the Good God,
Lord of the Two Lands, Ra . . . . . ., beloved
of Anubis of the North, endowed with life' etc.
as before. Osiris Temenos. Dyn. XII. and
XIII.

Pl. lix, 1. Fragment of an inscribed granite
block of Sebek-hotep III. The inscription
above the figure reads *neter nefer neb ȧri khet
Rȧ-khȧ-nefer se Rȧ mer-f Sebek-ḥetep de ȧnkh
zetta* 'The Good God, the Lord, Creator of
Things, Ra-kha-nefer, Son of the Sun, his
Beloved, Sebek-hotep, endowed with life for
ever.' The Horus-name *Ȧnkh-ȧb* appears.
Osiris Temple. Dyn. XIII.

2. A large, roughly-made, altar of offerings,
inscribed with the name of a person *Ȧd-ȧnekhen-
ȧd*, born of the lady *Mes-nekht[?]-ȧd*. Cemetery
G. Dyn. XI.

3. Two fragments of a limestone stele with
perpendicular lines of inscription, giving *seten
de ḥetep* formulae to Ptah-nefer-her and to
Hathor Lady of the House of Eternity, for the
kas of the *uȧrtu ne khaut ḥeqt Sebek-ḥetep maȧ
kheru* 'Secretary at the Royal Table, Sebek-
hotep, true-voiced'; and his wife, the *seten
kheker Nefert-uben* 'Royal Handmaid Nefert-
uben.' It should be mentioned here that the
female relatives of persons having the title
uȧrtu ne khaut ḥeqt very often hold the position
of *seten kheker*; and we may perhaps see a
direct conformity in the two titles, the one
being the male attendant upon the king, and
the other the female attendant upon the royal
hȧrem. Osiris Temenos. Dyn. XIII.

Pl. lx. 1. A limestone fragment, giving a
seten de ḥetep formula to *Usȧr neb Dedu neter
aȧ . . . . . neb ȧnkh ḥeq zetta.* 'Osiris, Lord
of Dedu, the Great God, ... Lord of Life,
Prince of Eternity,' that he may grant *per-
kheru*-offerings etc. for the *ka* of a certain
erpȧ ḥȧ Hereditary Prince, whose name is unfortunately missing. Osiris Temple. Dyn. XII.

2. An inscription in four perpendicular lines,
from the lap of a limestone kneeling figure of a
man. It reads (1) *Seten de ḥetep Usȧr neb
Ȧbdu de-f khet neb nefer uȧb per* (2) *ḥer khaut
ne Usȧr em khert ḥer net rȧ neb ne ka ne*
(3) *. . . . . y ḥeri dep aȧ ne Y . . . . . nebu
sȧḥu bȧti smer uȧti* (4) *erpȧt Ȧbdu mer sȧḥu*

uȧn tem em ȧḥȧ [?] *neb net seten per.* 'The King gives an offering to Osiris Lord of Abydos. May he grant all good and pure things, and a coming forth (2) upon the altar of Osiris at all times of the day, for the *ka* of (3) the . . . . ., Prince of all the . . . ., Royal Sealer, Chiefly Companion, (4) Heriditary Prince of Abydos, Superintendent of the Treasury, banishing the evil-doer at all times [?] from the Palace.' The last words of the inscription are given hypothetically, being founded on the supposition that the hieroglyphs read 𓄿𓏤𓈖𓇋𓄿𓅱𓅆𓏤𓊖𓉐. The sign 𓏏𓏏𓏏 at the beginning of the second line is an original error: it should be 𓉐. The name does not appear on the statue. Osiris Temple. Dyn. XII.

3. Portion of a limestone stele, giving the inscription [*m*]*er sȧḥu Ȧmeny maȧ kheru ȧri ne Set-Pepy maȧt kheru* 'The Superintendent of the Treasury, Ameny, deceased; born of Set-Pepy, true-voiced.' In the second line Ameny is called *mer per* 'Superintendent of the Palace'; and two other persons are mentioned, the one *sesh senb* 'the scribe Senb,' and the other *nebt per Set-Ḥether ȧrit ne Ȧ-ten* [?] 'The lady of the house, Set-Hathor, born of A-ten.' Osiris Temenos. Dyn. XIII.

4. Part of a limestone stele, upon which two lines of figures still remain. In the upper line, reading from left to right, these figures represent (i) *set-s seten kheker Nub-em-tekhi* 'Her daughter, the Royal Handmaid, Nub-em-tekhi'; (ii) *sen-f ur res met* [?] *sesh Renutet-se* 'His brother, the Great One of the Southern Tens, [?] the scribe, Renutet-se'; (iii) *set-s seten kheker Ȧmen-set* 'Her daughter, the Royal Handmaid, Amen-set'; (iv) *sen-f* [*ne*] *mut-* [*f ur*] *res met* [?] *Merit-ef* 'The brother of his mother, the Great One of the Southern Tens [?] Meritef'; and (v) *shems Pen-khenya* 'The attendant, Pen-khenya.' In the lower line the figures are (i) *sen-f sab er Nekhent Sebek-ḥetep mes ne*

Ȧmen-set 'His brother, the Judge belonging to the city of Nekhent, Sebek-hotep'; (ii) *set-s seten kheker Nub-khȧ-es* 'Her daughter, the Royal Handmaid, Nub-kha-es'; (iii) *sen-f uȧtu ne khaut ḥeq Sebek-ḥetep* 'His brother, the Secretary at the Royal Table, Sebek-hotep'; (iv) *her sesheta ne Ḥet-her nebt Annu Uȧh mes ne nebt per De-nub-merȧ* 'The master of the mysteries of Hathor Lady of Heliopolis, Uah: born of the lady of the house, De-nub-mera.' the hieroglyphs are so roughly cut that two of the above titles can only be translated hypothetically: 1 (ii) The original gives 𓄿𓈖𓏤, which seems to be a miswriting for 𓄿𓏤𓈖, shortly written 𓄿𓈖𓏤 *ur res met*; and 1 (iv) The original 𓈙𓏤𓏤 may perhaps be intended for the same title *ur res met*. Osiris Temple. Dyn. XIII.

5. Portion of an inscription from a broken limestone statuette, giving a *seten de ḥetep* formula for the *ka* of the *Erpȧ ḥȧ sȧḥu bȧti mer per* . . . . *Snȧȧ-ȧb maȧ kheru* 'Hereditary Prince, Royal Sealer, Superintendent of the Palace . . . . Snaa-ab, true-voiced.' By the coincidence of the names it would seem that this noble lived during the reign of Snaa-ab, a king of the XIIIth Dynasty, only known from a tablet found at Abydos. Osiris Temple. Dyn. XIII.

37. Pl. lxii. Limestone, coloured reliefs, giving the usual titles of Amenhotep I [*Zeser-ka-Rȧ*], and his father Ȧahmes I. Osiris Temple. Dyn. XVIII.

Pl. lxiii. Similar reliefs of king Amenhotep, which call for no special comment. Osiris Temple. Dyn. XVIII.

Pl. lxiv. In the middle of this plate is to be seen the great lintel of Tahutimes the Second and Third. In the three horizontal lines the inscriptions commence from the central 𓋹, and read to left and right. The left hand side is as follows: (1) *Ankh Ḥer ka em Uast* (2) *Seten bȧti neb taui Rȧ-men-kheper mȧ Rȧ* (3) *se Rȧ*

ne _khat-f Tahut-mes-nefer-kheperu_ zetta (1) 'The
living Horus, Bull in Thebes, (2) King of Upper
and Lower Egypt, Lord of the two Lands,
Ra-men-kheper, (3) Son of the Sun, of his
body, Tahutimes-nefer-kheperu (the Third),
like the Sun for ever.' The right hand
side gives the cartouches _Rá-aá-kheper-ne_
and _Tahut-mes-nefer-kháu_ (the Second),
with similar titles. Osiris Temple. Dyn.
XVIII.

Pl. lxv. 9, 10. Standing figures of a man and
woman, roughly worked in grey granite, having
two vertical lines of hieroglyphs upon the front
and back. The frontal inscriptions read: _neter
hen dep ne Usár Un-nefer maá kheru_; and _sent-f
nebt per-f qemát ne Ast Thiy_ 'The High Priest
of Osiris, Un-nefer, true-voiced; his sister, the
lady of his house, the Singer of Isis, Thiy.'
That upon the back reads: _Se-hez Usár neter
hen dep ne Usár Un-nefer maá kheru; nebt per-f
qemát Usár Thiy maát kheru zed nes Nefert-ári_
'The glorified Osirian High Priest of Osiris, Un-
nefer, true-voiced; the lady of his house, the
Singer of Osiris, Thiy, true-voiced, also named
[lit. said of her] Nefertari.' A few notes with
regard to the life of this famous High Priest
are given in connection with two other of his
inscriptions upon pl. lxvii. Osiris Temenos.
Dyn. XIX.

Pl. lxvi. 1. Fragment of a small limestone
stele, upon which a man is figured, holding in
his hand a kind of brazier. Above his head is
inscribed . . . . . _per hen-f . . . u-nefer Ámen-
neb uhem ánkh_ '. . . of the palace of . His
Majesty [in] the city of . . . . . u-nefer:
Amen-neb, renewing life.' Osiris Temenos.
Dyn. XVIII.

2. Portion of a limestone stele of a man and
his sister. The name of the former is destroyed,
but that of the latter is Bakt-mut. Osiris
Temenos. Dyn. XIX.

3. Two fragments of a limestone statuette
of a person named . . . . . _yá_, giving the
interesting invocation _áau ne ka-k Usár_ 'Adora-

tions to thy _ka_, O Osiris.' Osiris Temenos.
Dyn. XIX.

4. Two fragments of the inscription upon a
small basalt statuette of Min-mes, the High
Priest of Anhur. Min-mes, who is known from
various other monuments (GARSTANG, _El Arabah_,
pp. 11, 35; _Proc. Soc. Bib. Arch._ vol. xxiii,
p. 250; _idem_ p. 13), lived in the reign of
Rameses II, and was the step-brother of the
High Priest of Osiris, Un-nefer, who is mentioned in this chapter. Early in life he held
the positions of royal scribe, and priest of Shu
and of Anhur: his father _Herá_ being High
Priest of the latter deity. He was later elevated
by Rameses to the position of _ámi as Shu
Tefnut_ 'Official of the Temple of Shu and
Tefnut; and on his father's death became High
Priest of Anhur. A statuette calls him _kheri
heb heri dep ne neb taui_ 'Chief Lector to the
King.' The Lectors seem to have corresponded
in a manner to the Magi of Persia; and the
position of Chief Lector, although at this
period much deteriorated, was in the Old
Kingdom one of the highest in the land.
Dyn. XIX.

5. Part of a limestone stele, showing a seated
male figure holding a lotus flower. At the top
is a short inscription reading . . . . _ne ka ne
ákhu áker Rá neb pet seten neteru Pa-ási_ '. . . .
for the _ka_ of the perfect glory of Ra, Lord of
Heaven, King of the Gods: Pa-asi.' A some-
what similar stele of this person, whereon his
name is written [hieroglyphs], has just been
published by M. Capart in his 'Recueil de
Monuments Égyptiens, 1902.' He is there
called the [hieroglyphs] 'glory of Ra.' Professor Maspero has several times called attention to the formula _ne ka ne ákhu áker ne
Rá_, and he remarks that this apparent identification of the deceased with Ra occurs in a few
inscriptions of the XIXth and XXth Dynasties,
but at no other period. There is a Pa-asi
known on a papyrus at Turin, who held the

position of Commander of the Troops, and M. Capart thinks that an identification may be possible. Osiris Temple. Dyn. XIX.

6. Portion of a limestone stele inscribed *Ȧri ne zat ne Ȧmen Keni-Ȧmen maȧ kheru* 'Born of the standard-bearer of Amen, Keni-Amen, true-voiced.' The stele evidently contained originally the figure of the son of Keni-Amen as well. Osiris Temple. Dyn. XIX.

7. Limestone stele upon which five persons are depicted seated before a table of offerings. Above them there are the remains of a group of gods. At the bottom of the stele two lines of hieroglyphs give a *seten de ḥetep* formula to *Usȧr Khent Ȧmenta neb Ta-zeser* 'Osiris Khent-amenti, Lord of the Necropolis,' that he may grant *per kheru* offerings for the *ka* of the *Seten uḥem dep ne neb taui semȧ medetu ȧdebui Khȧy* 'Chief Royal Herald of the Lord of the Two Lands, reporting the countries' affairs: Khay.' Elsewhere we see that his father was named ⬜🦅𓏤🦆 *Haȧ* or ⬜🦅𓏤🦆𓏤 *Haȧa*, and bore the titles *sab* 'Judge,' and *ḥer ṛezetu ne neter nefer* 'Commander of the King's archers.' His sister was the *nebt per Im-ȧ-mer* 'Lady of the house, Imamer'; and his mother the *qemȧt ne Ȧmen nebt per Nub-em-tekh* 'Singer of Amen, the Lady of the house, Nub-em-tekh.' Another personage holds the title *mer shenuti* 'Superintendent of the Granary,' but his name and relationship is lost. Osiris Temenos. Dyn. XIX.

Pl. lxvii, 1. Limestone statue with seven horizontal lines of hieroglyphs, each line beginning with a *seten de ḥetep* formula. The first is to the gods Ra-Harmakhis and Tum, that they may grant *nefu* 'breezes' to the *ka* of the deceased; the second to *Usȧr khent enti er Amentet* 'Osiris, the Chief who is [existent] in the Underworld,' that he may grant the usual funeral offerings; the third to *Usȧr Un-nefer neb ta-zeser* 'Osiris Unnefer, Lord of the Necropolis,' without a prayer. The fourth line is to

Anpu [en]ti neter Ded 'Anubis, who is the god of Ded' (the original 🐕🔺𓎺𓏢 is a sculptor's error for 𓃣𓏤𓎺𓏢, a common title of Anubis), that he may grant *ḥesu em baḥ seten* 'Favour in the presence of the King' for the *ka*. The fifth line to *Ȧnpu neb rekh* 'Anubis, Lord of knowledge,' praying for *ḥȧ nefer shems ne ka-f* 'a goodly tomb, and a following for his *ka*'; the sixth to Osiris, that he may grant *ȧkhu em pet usr em ta maȧ kheru em set maȧt* 'Glory in heaven, power on earth, and a trueness of voice in the Place of Justice' [the 𓊪𓎺 is a miswriting for 𓊪𓎺 undoubtedly]; and the seventh to *Usȧr neb ta-zeser Ȧnpu ȧmi em ut* 'Osiris Lord of the Necropolis, and Anubis dwelling in embalmment,' that they may grant *shems Seker* 'a following of the god Seker' for the *ka*. The name and titles of the owner appear at the end of each line, and in other parts of the statue, and read, when written in full, *Mer kau emt ḥet Rȧ-usr-maȧ-setep-ne-Rȧ Ȧmen em per Ptaḥ-em-uaḥ maȧ kheru* 'Superintendent of the Cattle in the Temple of Ramessu II, in the Amen Temple, Ptaḥ-em-uaḥ, true-voiced. This building, which is still to be seen at Abydos, is known as the Rameses Temple, and stands near to the great Temple of Sety. In one place Ptah-em-uah is called *seten sesh ḥetep neter ne neteru nebu* 'the royal scribe of the divine offerings of all the gods.' The cartouches of Ramessu II are inscribed upon the sides of the statue. Osiris Temenos. Dyn. XIX.

2. Wooden fragment with an inscription, giving a prayer for the welfare of an untitled person named Bay. Cemetery G. Dyn. XIX.

3. Part of a limestone stele, upon which two figures are represented in attitudes of worship. Above them is a much damaged inscription, reading, as far as can now be seen, *seten sesh ne per aȧ Ur-maȧu maȧ kheru ȧri ne . . . . . . y* 'The Royal Scribe of Pharaoh, Urmaau, true-voiced, born of . . . . . . y.' Osiris Temple. Dyn. XIX.

38. Pl. lxvii. 4. Two fragments from small basalt statuettes of Un-nefer, High Priest of Osiris in the reign of Rameses II. The first inscription reads (1) *neter ḥen dep ne Usȧr Un-nefer maȧ kheru* (2) *sem ḥet Seḳeri Un-nefer maȧ kheru* 'The High Priest of Osiris, Un-nefer, true-voiced; the *sem*-priest of the Temple of Seker, Un-nefer, true-voiced.' The 𓊹𓄿 *sem*-priesthood is very little understood, but it was evidently of a mystical character. The *sem*-priest officiated at the most solemn ceremonies, such, for instance, as the 'opening of the mouth' of a mummy, where he performed the chief part; and at many other of the more occult services he took a leading place. The 𓉐 Temple, or Sanctuary, of Seker was that portion of the Temple of Sety known in Mariette's *Abydos* as Salle T. In the inscriptions upon the temple walls we find it constantly mentioned, being sometimes written 𓉐 and sometimes 𓉐. Once the following invocation occurs 𓀭𓈖𓏏𓉐 *Usȧr Un-nefer ḥer ȧb ḥet Seker de-f ȧnkh usr ne Rȧ-men-maȧt* 'May Osiris-Unnefer within the Sanctuary of Seker grant life and power to Ra-men-maat [Sety I].' The second fragment gives an extremely interesting title. It appears to read *mer zazanut ne maȧ kheru Un-nefer maȧ kheru* 'Superintendent of the judicial court of the true-voiced, Un-nefer, true-voiced.' The word 𓏭, 𓏭, or 𓏭 *zazanut* signifies a court or office, usually of a judicial character; and Unnefer's title 'Superintendent of the court of the True of Voice [*maȧ kheru*, i.e. the dead]' seems to be to some extent the religious equivalent of the judicial title 'Superintendent of the royal *zazanut* court of the deliberating upon all words' (vide MAR., *Mast.*, 109; ERMAN, *Life in A. E.*, 138). Osiris Temple. Dyn. XIX.

As we have thus had three inscriptions of this Unnefer, who was perhaps the most important of the inhabitants of Abydos of all ages, it may be as well to mention a few points with regard to his life and family. Unnefer was born probably in the reign of Sety I, as he appears to have been an elderly man in the reign of Ramessu II. He began his sacerdotal career as a priest of Osiris, in which position he appears on the shrine found this year by the Egyptian Research Account, near the Sety Temple. Later he became, as we have seen, the *sem*-priest of the Sanctuary of Seker in that building; and also received the position, which we have just discussed, in connection with the *Maȧ Kheru*. He finally became High Priest of Osiris at Abydos, and caused himself to be remembered by filling the temple with statues, statuettes, and steles, inscribed with his name and titles. With regard to his father there was evidently an unpleasant mystery. On nearly all his later monuments when his parentage is given he is said to be the son of the High Priest of Osiris, Meri, and of his wife the Singer of Osiris, Mȧ-ȧa-nuy. But on one or two statues his father is said to be the High Priest of Osiris Yu-yu, and on the above mentioned shrine the name Meri is, in each of the three places where it occurs, erased, and the name Yu-yu substituted. Unnefer married the lady Thiy whose second name was Nefert-ari; and by her he had several children, whose names are given [?] on a monument found in his tomb at Abydos, and not yet published. His two step-brothers are to be noticed: the one is Pa-rȧ-ḥetep the Vizīr, and the other Min-mes, the High Priest of Anhur, mentioned on pl. lxvi. They were the sons of Mȧ-aa-nuy by Ḥerȧ, High Priest of Anhur, the son of Un-nefer, High Priest of Amen. The base of a statuette of this Hera was found this year at Abydos, but was stolen almost immediately by some loafers from the village. A portion of the extensive genealogy of Unnefer may be given here, as it illustrates also the family positions of Min-mes and Herȧ.

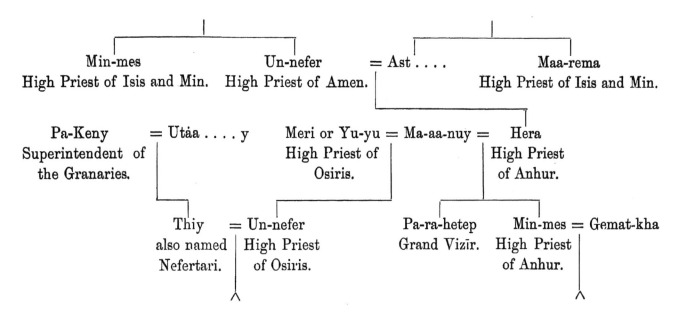

5. Upon this plate there still remain two inscriptions to be discussed. They are cut upon natural limestone rocks lying in the desert, between the village of El Arâbah and the site of the Royal Tombs. The longer reads *Neter ḥen IV ne Åmen-Rå seten neteru mer res nut må kedes Menṯhu-em-ḥåt maå kheru.* 'The 4th Priest of Amen-Ra, King of the Gods, Superintendent of Thebes in its entirety, Mentuemhat, true-voiced.' The other reads *Neter ḥen IV ne Åmen-Rå, seten neteru mer [res nut] Menṯhu-em-ḥåt* 'The 4th Priest of Amen-Ra, King of the Gods, Superintendent [of Thebes] Mentuemhat.' It would seem that Mentuemhat came to Abydos to inspect the royal tombs, and had his name roughly inscribed upon one of the rocks near by: the inscription being re-written more neatly, and at greater length, with the addition of *maå kheru* also, after his death. Mentuemhat, it will be remembered, was the great vizir at the time of the Assyrian invasions of Egypt. Besides the above titles he held the offices of *Ḥå*-Prince of Thebes, Great Prince [ ] of the Temple, Instructor of the Priests, Superintendent of the Priests of Mentu, *Ḥeq*-Prince of the Desert [ ], Superintendent of the Frontier [ ] etc. etc. He was the son of Nes-

Ptah, governor of Thebes, but was probably of Cypriote origin, as a wonderfully carved portrait-head—found by Miss Benson and Miss Gourlay in the Temple of Mut—inscribed with his titles, seems to show (see NEWBERRY in *Temple of Mut*, p. 352). Of him Miss Gourlay writes "He probably helped Taharqa [in whose reign he lived] to repel the first Assyrian invasion; nevertheless, after the conquest of Upper Egypt and the sack of Thebes by Assurbanipal, he still retained his position as governor of the Thebaid. . . . When the withdrawal of the Assyrian invaders left him free to exercise his governorship, he devoted himself to the restoration of the broken and pillaged temples, and of the worship and festivals of the gods . . . . These pious labours . . . were wholly swept away in the second invasion of Assurbanipal and the consequent ruin of the city. No record has yet been found to show whether after that catastrophe he still retained his governorship and painfully attempted a second restoration of the desecrated shrines, or whether his career then came to an end with that of the dynasty he served." Our inscription, however, which seems to show that he was powerful to the end of his life, suggests that he did attempt a second restoration; and indeed the strength portrayed in his face is a guarantee of his ability to undertake such a task, however painful it was. Dyn. XXVI.

39. Pl. lxix. 1. Limestone altar of offerings, around the edge of which run *seten de hetep* formulae to 'Osiris, Chief of the Underworld, Great Lord of Abydos,' and to 'Osiris, Lord of Dedu, Great Lord of Abydos,' for the *ka* of the *mer sāhutiu Her āri ne Set-Het-her* 'Superintendent of the Treasuries, Hor, born of Set-Hathor.' Osiris Temenos. Dyn. XXVI.

2. Limestone altar of offerings, around which is inscribed twice the following. *Ānkh Her smen maāt sma uti Net se sepd taui Her nub neteru setep seten bāti Rā-uāh-āb se Rā Āahmes-net-se Usār khent Āmentet neter aā neb Ābdu meri de ānkh Rā mā zetta.* 'The Living Horus, establishing Truth, Lord of the Vulture and the Uraeus, Son of Neith, the Vigour of the two Lands, the Golden Horus, Chosen of the Gods, the King of Upper and Lower Egypt, Ra-uah-ab, Son of the Sun Ahmes-net-se, beloved of Osiris Lord of the Underworld, the Great God, Lord of Abydos, endowed with Life, like the Sun for ever.' Osiris Temenos. Dyn. XXVI.

Pl. lxxi. Portions of a painted wooden coffin, inscribed with religious texts, too fragmentary to be translated with interest. The owner's name is Tahuti-mes, but his only title is 'scribe.' Cemetery G. Dyn. XVIII—XX.

Pl. lxxii, 1. Painted wooden canopic box, inscribed down either side with *seten de hetep* formulae to Anubis, that he may grant *ākhu ne pet kher Rā usr em ta* . . . . 'glory in heaven under Ra, and power on earth . . . ,' and the usual funeral offerings of beer, bulls, geese, etc., to the *ka* of the owner, whose name, *Merti-heru*, appears in the centre. Cemetery G. About Dyn. XXVIII.

2. The model coffin figured upon this plate belongs to the same personage, as also does a coffin represented upon the next plate. Upon the one side he is called the *hesi-ka* priest, and *āmi ās* [a kind of priest], and is said to be the

son of the *nebt per Nes-her* 'Lady of the house, Nesher.' Upon the other side a curious inscription occurs, reading *dep-k āb-k ānkh-k āmi-f* 'Thy head, thy heart, thy life are in it' [*i.e.* in the coffin]. The signs here transliterated *āb-k*, are in the original ⌐○⌐, which might perhaps be rendered 'thy first, or chiefest, thing.' But it seems more probable that the group is a mis-writing for ♡⌐ *āb-k* 'thy heart.'

Pl. lxxiii, 1. The coffin of Merti-heru gives us some more details, with regard to his family. He was the son of a person holding the same titles as himself, named *Uāh-āb-Rā*; and his mother, as stated above, was named Nes-her, and held the title *āhyt ne khent enti Āmentet* 'Sistrum player of the Chief who is in the Underworld,' *i.e.* Osiris. Cemetery G. About Dyn. XXVIII.

40. Pl. lxxiii, 2. The coffin of Tay-nekht has the following genealogical inscription: *Usār Tay-nekht set āmi ās Zed-her mes ne nebt per Ta-kherd-ne-Min* 'The Osirian Tay-nekht, daughter of the *āmi ās* priest Zedher, and of the lady of the house, Ta-kherd-ne-Min.' The text of these inscriptions is unimportant, and is so corrupt that it is unnecessary to translate it in full. Cemetery G. Dyn. XXX.

3. The coffin of Heru-makheru speaks of him as *Usār Her-maā-kheru maā-kheru se Merit-heru mes ne nebt per Mehti-[āb?]-ta-senekht* 'The Osirian Heru-makheru, deceased, son of Merit-heru, and of the Lady of the house Mehti-ab-ta-senekht.' There seems to be no doubt that the signs ∽ should be read ∽ *mehti-āb*—the common expression 'filling, or pleasing, the heart.' Cemetery G. Dyn. XXX.

4. The box of Tasenmeht doubtless belonged to this same lady. Her name is here written ⌐🦅〰️🎐𓀒, but this is an obvious error for ⌐🦅〰️𓀒 Mehti-ab-ta-senekht. Cemetery G. Dyn. XXX.

5. The inscription on the coffin of Mert-tefnut

reads *Mert-tefnut maåt kheru set ne åmi ås ḥesi ka Zedher* 'Mert-tefnut, deceased, daughter of the *åmi ås* and *ḥesi ka*-priest Zedher.' Cemetery G. Dyn. XXX.

6. The gilt cartonnage of Neb-ta-ahit has inscribed upon it *Usår Neb-ta-åhy[t] maåt kheru set neter ḥen seten sesh Nefer-åb-Rå* [?] *maå-kheru, mes ne Tå . . . .* [?] 'The Osirian Neb-ta-ahyt, true-voiced, daughter of the priest and royal scribe Nefer-ab-Ra, true-voiced, and of Ta . . . .' Cemetery G. Dyn. XXX.

Pl. lxxv, 1. The inscription of Nefert-iut speaks of her as *Usår qemåt khent Åmentet Nefert-iut . . . .* 'The Osirian, Singer of Khent-amenti, Nefert-iut.' Cemetery G. Dyn. XXX.

2. The sarcophagus of Hapi-men is inscribed with a *seten de ḥetep* formula to *Usår khent Åmentet neter aå neb Åbdu* 'Osiris, Khent-Amenti, the Great God, Lord of Abydos,' that he may grant the usual offerings for the *ka* of the *neter ḥen III ne Mut nebt em Åben* [?] *neter ḥen Ḥer Usår Hapi-men maå kheru* 'The 3rd Priest of Mut Lady in Aben, Priest of Horus, the Osirian Hapi-men, true-voiced.' The town ⸗ *Åb* or *Åben* is unknown. Cemetery G. Dyn. XXX.

The two middle inscriptions are from the sarcophagi of the brothers Peduenast and Horuza. That of the former gives a prayer to Osiris on behalf of the *neter ḥen Un sesh ne neter pen Ḥer ån mut-f Pe-de-ne-åst maå kheru se neter ḥen Ḥet-ḥer nebt Ånt mert* [?] *Rå Zed-ḥer maå kheru årit ne nebt per Neb-ta-åhyt maåt kheru* 'Priest of Un, Scribe of this God [*i.e.* the King], Horus Supporter of his Mother,[1] Peduenast, true-voiced; son of the Priest of Hathor Lady of Ant, the Eye of Ra, Zed-her, true-voiced; born of the Lady of the House Neb-ta-ahyt, true-voiced.'

4. The latter inscription gives a longer prayer to Osiris, for the *neter ḥen Un sesh Per-aå åu-f åpi* [*ḥetepu?*] *ne neter pen per neb uazeti Ånt Ḥeruza maå kheru se neter ḥen Ḥet-ḥer nebt Ånt mert* [?] *Rå Zed-ḥer maå kheru årit ne nebt per Neb-ta-åhyt maåt kheru* 'Priest of Un, Scribe of Pharaoh, counting [the offerings] of this god in every temple in Uazeti-Ant, Heruza, true-voiced; son of the Priest of Hathor Lady of Ant, the Eye of Horus, Zed-her, true-voiced; born of the Lady of the House, Neb-ta-ahyt, true-voiced.' In this inscription there are a few points to be noticed. The sentence [hieroglyphs] *åu-f åpi ne neter pen* seems to require an additional word, such as *ḥetepu* 'offerings,' to complete the sense. The words [hieroglyphs] *neter pen per neb* are also written [hieroglyphs] towards the close of the inscription, which seems to be erroneous. The [hieroglyphs] *neter ḥen Un sesh Per-aå*, or [hieroglyphs] *neter ḥen Un sesh ne neter pen* as it is written upon the sarcophagus of Pedu-enast, may be translated as above; but the fact that the god [hieroglyph] *Un* is very rarely found[2] urges the necessity of another reading to the passage. Regarding *un* as the auxiliary verb, it might be rendered 'The Priest, being the Scribe of the King'; or again it has been suggested that the word should be read [hieroglyph] *un* 'opening,' thus giving the sense 'the Priest, opening the writings of the King.' But the corruption of the whole text makes a close translation impossible. Cemetery G. Dyn. XXX.

41. Pl. lxxvi. Three bronze hypocephali, decorated with the usual magical figures and inscriptions. The latter are hopelessly confused;

---

[1] For this title see CRUM, *Proc. Soc. Bib. Arch.* 1894, xvi, 131; BREASTED, *New Chapter in Life of Tahutmes III.*, p. 12; and GRIFFITH in *Deshasheh*, p. 47.

[2] Un is mentioned in the leading hieroglyphical dictionaries without references, and it is doubtful whether there is such a god.

many of the groups of signs bearing but a faint resemblance, if any at all, to known words. Although there are some thirty specimens in the various museums, a comparison of these with the present ones does not help much in their decipherment; and it would therefore be very undesirable to offer even a conditional translation. Such an one, however, giving an idea of the style of the texts should be referred to in Dr. Budge's *Egyptian Magic*, page 119. Of the three hypocephali the third alone bears the name of the person for whom it was made. This reads

Usár neter hen Zed-her maá kheru mes nebt per Uza-áu maát kheru 'The Osirian priest Zed-her, true-voiced, born of the Lady of the House Uza-au, true-voiced.'

The hypocephalus appears to have had its origin in connection with chapter clxii of the *Book of the Dead*. From the rubric of this chapter we learn that a figure of the cow Hathor was to be fashioned in gold, and placed upon the neck of the mummy; and that another was to be drawn upon papyrus, and placed under the head, the idea being to give "warmth" to the deceased in the underworld. After the XXVIth Dynasty the cow-amulet fell into disuse, and the drawing upon papyrus developed into the hypocephalus, upon which the cow always remained an important figure. Papyrus was almost entirely abandoned in favour of more durable material, such as linen, stucco, and rarely bronze. The fashion, however was not long-lived, and did not survive the fall of the XXXth Dynasty.

Taking the largest specimen as an example, the figures are as follows. First line: *Nehebka* holding the *uzat* eye. Although here pictured as an ape, Nehebka is in reality the serpent-god whose worship was carried on at Heracleopolis. He stands, here, in front of the seated figure of Horus-Min, behind whom is an *uzat*-headed goddess. Then follow the cow of Hathor, and

the four genii of the dead. Behind these there is an interesting group, consisting of a lotus, a lion, and a ram, which occurs in chapter clxii of the *Book of the Dead* [line 5] in the form. Following this group is a pylon crowned with the head of Khnemu; the god Horus-Ra holding the ⚡ *ánkh*; and finally the *kheper* or scarabeus. Second line: the Sun-boat navigated by Horus and two apes, Isis and Nephthys being conspicuous among the occupants; the youthful Horus seated above the tempest [?]; the Moon-boat steered by Harpocrates; and the goddess Nut and scarabeus. Turning the hypocephalus round we notice the Four-headed ram-god, in whom the spirits of the four elements, Ra [fire], Shu [air], Geb [earth], and Usár [water] were said to be united.[1] In this form the god was worshipped at Mendes; and an inscription[2] speaks of him as the 'Fourfold god in the land of Mendes,' *Ánep* being his shrine in that city. Two small apes, the final degradation of the eight adoring cynocephali may be noticed. These represent the four primeval pairs of gods of chaos, whose names were Nun and Nunt [moisture], Hehu and Hehut [air], Kekui and Kekuit [darkness], Gereh and Gereht [rest]; being called collectively *Khemenu*,[3] a miswriting of. Above, there are three boats: the first contains Horus, the second Horus-Sept, and the third Khepera. Finally there is the double god who personified the rising and setting of the sun. Figures such as these just described are to be found on nearly all the known hypocephali, however erratic the inscriptions. Nevertheless, as may be seen from the two

---

[1] BRUGSCH, *Thes.* 4te Abt. 734 *et seq.*
[2] *Ibid., Oase*, pl. xxvi. l. 27.
[3] *Ibid., Thes.* 4te Abt. 672-3.

smaller specimens, they may be greatly cut down, and are subject to much degradation of form.[1] Cemetery G. Dyn. XXX.

42. Besides the above inscriptions there are one or two which may be noted, taken from steles and other objects so much damaged as not to have been worth preserving.

1. Limestone stele, originally coloured. A figure is represented standing before a table of offerings, and the accompanying inscription,

above and in front of it, reads *Seten de ḥetep Usȧr neb D[edu]* . . . . *ȧmakhu kher neter aȧ* . . . . *khet neb nefer uȧbt ne ka ne sȧḥu bȧti smer uȧti Ȧ* . . . *em-ḥetep ren-f nefer* . . . . 'The King gives an offering to Osiris Lord of Dedu . . . . reverence with the great god . . . . all good and pure things, for the *ka* of the Royal Sealer, the Chiefly Companion, A . . . em-hotep, surnamed . . . . .' Cemetery G. Dyn. XI.

2. Limestone stele in three divisions, of which the two lower are destroyed. In the upper portion three figures sit before a table of offerings. The first represents a male named *Ankh ȧt ȧri ne Sba* 'Ankh-at, born of Sba'; the second a female

named . . . . *ḥetep ȧri ne Sba* '. . . . hotep, born of Sba'; and the third a male whose name is destroyed. Around the edges there are *seten de ḥetep* formulae to Osiris Lord of Abydos, and [Anpu] Lord of Ta-zeser, that they may grant *per kheru* offerings to the *Kas*. Osiris Temple. Dyn. XIII.

3. Remains of a limestone stele, inscribed *se ne . . . sesh ḥesebtu uȧb ne Usȧr Un-nefer . . .* 'Son of the scribe of the accounts, the *uȧb-*

priest of Osiris Un-nefer . . .' The rest of the long inscription is completely obliterated. Cemetery G. Dyn. XVI.

4. Painted wooden box, now fallen to pieces, of Heru-maakheru, who is mentioned on plate lxxiii. It was inscribed as follows:—

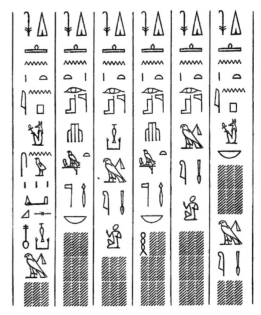

As will be seen, it gives *seten de ḥetep* formulae to Osiris and Anpu for the benefit of the Osirian *hesi-ka*-priest Heru-maakheru. Cemetery G. About Dyn. XXVIII.

---

[1] Reference should be made to: *Proc. Soc. Bib. Arch.* vol. vi, 37, 52, 126, 129, 170, 185, 187; vol. vii, 213; vol. xix, 146. LIEDEMANN, *Religion*, p. 298. *Rev. Arch.* 1862, vi, 129. *Archaeol.* xxxvi, 1855, 163. *Catalogue of Edinburgh Nat. Mus.* 1900, p. 8. LEEMANS, in *Trav. du Congrès des Orientalistes à Leide*, 1884. *Catalogue of Turin Mus.*

INDEX.

Aahmes I, portrait of 30
   ,, II. 30, 31
   ,, ,, called *se Asar* 32
   ,, ,, cartouches of 32
Ab, scribe. 29
  ,, Aben, city. 49
Ab amulet 39
Ad or Adu 27, 41
Adzes of copper 23
  ,, model 30
Aegean pottery of Ist Dyn. 6
  ,, ,, ,, ,, date confirmed . 6
A . . . . . em-hotep 51
Agathodaemon 25
Ahyt of Khentamenti 48
Akhenaten, erasure of cartouches by . . 30
Alabaster, carved 7
  ,, vases . . . 6, 7, 16, 17, 18, 34
  ,, in foundation deposits . . 32, 33
Alphabetic marks 23
Altars of offerings . . . 29, 32, 42, 48
Amenhotep I 30
  ,, ,, portrait of 30
  ,, ,, temple of 30
  ,, II, Ka-name of 30
  ,, ,, *Sed* festival of . . . 30
  ,, III, glazed plaque of . . . 31
Amen-neb. 44
Ameny 29, 43
Ami as 48, 49
Amulets 23, 24, 25, 37, 38, 39
  ,, original order of 38
Anhur 28, 41, 44, 47
Animals chipped in flint 12
Ankh 25
Ankh-at 51
Antef I, figure of 28
  ,, ,, temple of 28
  ,, V 9
  ,, ,, architrave of 28
  ,, ,, columns of 28, 41

Anubis 42, 45, 51
  ,, represented 36
Ap—Ka 3
Ap, Apa 3
Ape 25, 50
Architrave of Antef V 28
  ,, ,, Tahutmes III . . . 30
Arrow-head, ivory 24
  ,, bronze 25
Assa. 28
Auhet-abu, Queen 29, 31
Axes of copper 23
  ,, model 30
Azab 3, 8
  ,, inscription of 5

Baboons, green glazed 25
Bakt-mut 44
Bay 31, 45
Bead, lazuli, of Psamtek 25
Beads 16, 18, 24, 25, 34, 38
  ,, carnelian 18
  ,, network of 36, 40
  ,, packet of 16
Beard, ebony 36
Beetle, serpentine 23
Bener-ab, bracelet of 5
Beryl amulets 38
Bird-bones 18
Bird-bone, pattern on 7
Bird, limestone 25
Birds on tree, painted 23
  ,, on trial-piece 31
Black incised pottery, foreign . . . 5
Black-topped ,, ... 6
Blue glass fish 31
Bone netter 18, 24
  ,, splint, broken 38
Bones 39
  ,, disturbed at burial . . . 17, 18
  ,, loose in grave 39

Book of the Dead 38, 50
Borer of copper 7
Box, canopic 35, 36, 38, 40, 48
Bracelets, flint 16
   ,,   ivory 5
   ,,   shell 17
   ,,   slate 17
Brazier 44
Breccia pediment 34
Broken splint bone 38
Bronze arrowhead 25
   ,, figures of gods 32
   ,, hypocephali 38
Bulbous root 36
Bull's head amulets 23, 25
   ,,   ,, foundation deposits . . 32
Burial, cut-up 17, 18
Burials, undisturbed 18
Buto, city 41
Button 24

Canopic box . . . 35, 36, 38, 40, 48
Carnelian amulets 38
   ,,   beads 18
   ,,   in foundation deposits . . 32, 33
Cartonnage 36, 38, 49
Cartouche of Aahmes II 32
   ,,   ,, Mer-en-ra 41
   ,,   ,, Nectanebo I . . . 33
   ,,   ,,   ,, II . . . 33
   ,,   erased 29, 30, 42
   ,,   plaques 32
Carved alabaster 7
   ,,   ivory 5
   ,,   slate 5
   ,,   wood 7
Caulfeild, A. St. G. 2
Cemetery, G. 1, 34
   ,,   ,, inscriptions . . 42, 48—51
Chisel, copper 23
Christie, H. L. 2
Clay coffins 15
   ,, sealing of Ro 4
   ,,   ,, Shepseskaf . . . 27
Cobble paving in graves 17
Coffins, clay 15
   ,, model 35, 36, 48
   ,, wood 35, 36, 38
Coloured scenes 30
Comb flints 12
Commander of archers 42, 45
   ,,   troops 45

Construction of tombs 15, 36, 37
Contracted burial 15, 35
Copper adze 23, 30
   ,,   axe 23, 30
   ,,   borer 7
   ,,   chisel 23
   ,,   cutting-out tool 23
   ,,   in foundation deposits . . 30, 32, 33
Correlation of dating of remains . . 19—22
Counterpoise or *menat* 30
Crescent flints 12, 26
Crocodile, flint 23
   ,,   bone 25
Crystal cup 5
Cubit of slate 25
   ,, division of 25
Cursive writing, earliest 3, 4
Cutting-out tools 23
Cut-up burial 17, 18
Cylinder 23, 24
   ,,   ivory 24
   ,,   jars 19, 22, 23
   ,,   seal 23

Da-Khnum 7
Dating of tombs . . . . . 19—21
   ,, of flints 8, 11, 12
   ,,   pottery 6
   ,,   *ushabtiu* 38, 39
Decease shown by *menat*, counterpoise . 30
Den 4, 6, 15
   ,, flints of 12
Dep, city 41
Deposits, foundation 30, 32
   ,,   materials of . . 32
Direction of tombs 15
Dog (?) mummy 40
Dolomite vases, gold-capped . . . 7
Draughtsman, ivory 24
Drawing of flints 2, 10
   ,,   inscriptions . . . 2
   ,,   pottery 12
Du as variant for *da* 8
Dwarf, drawing of 5

Erased cartouches XIIIth Dyn. . . 29, 42
   ,,   ,, XVIIIth Dyn. . . 30
Erpa 43
   ,, *ha* 41, 42, 43
Errors in hieroglyphs . . . 41, 43, 45, 48

False doors 27, 41
   „ fringe 5
Felspar, green, in foundation deposits . . . 32
Fire-rings, pottery 25
Fish, blue glass 31
Fish-hook 24
Flakes, flint 8, 12, 25
Flint animals 12
   „ bracelets 16
   „ combs 12
   „ core 11
   „ crescents 12
   „ disc 11
   „ flakes 8, 12, 25
   „ hoes 11
   „ knives 8, 10, 11, 16
   „   „ wear of 11
   „ saws 12
   „ scrapers 7, 8, 11
   „ working in successive reigns . . . 8
Floor-supports 14
Forehead pendants 23
Forked lance, model 24
   „   „ connection with *Pesh-ken* amulet . 24
Foundation deposits, materials of . . . 30, 32
   „   „ of Tahutmes III . . . 30
Furniture 31
   „ temple 25

Gazelle 16, 17
Genealogies 35, 47
Genii, four 36, 38, 39, 40, 50
   „ holding knives 36
Glass amulets 38
   „ fish 31
   „ in foundation deposits 32
Glaze, green, in foundation deposits . . 31, 32
Glazed quartz 25
Glory of Ra 44
God, Min, ink-drawn 4
Gold cap 25
   „ capped vases 7
Gold foil *hotep* mat 6
   „ ornaments 31
   „ ring 34
   „ strip of Aha 8
Grains of corn 32
Granite head 28
   „ pylon 27
   „ shrine 32
Great One of Southern Tens 43

Green felspar in foundation deposits . . . 32
Grinders, stone . . . . . 12, 25—6

Ha, Queen 3
Ha sign 4
Ha prince of Thebes 47
Haa-ab-ra, plaque of 32
Haematite 16
   „ amulets . . . . . , . 38
Hall, pillared, XVIIIth Dyn. 29
Hammer-stones . . . . . , . 18
Hapi-men 39, 49
Hathor 43
   „ cow of 50
Haunches 32
Hawk, mummy 39
Hay, Hayt 3
Head, granite 28
   „ jasper 31
   „ quartzite 32
   „ steatite 31
Heart scarab 39
Hem sign 4
Hemi-discs of alabaster 32, 33
Heq 28, 42
Her dep aa 47
Heru, seal-bearer 32
Heru-maa-kheru 35, 36
Hesi-ka priest 48, 49, 51
Hieroglyphic inscriptions, oldest known . . 3, 4
Hippopotamus' head 26
Hoes, flint 11
Hora, limestone figure of 31
Horn cup of Mena 7
Hor-nub, title 41, 48
Horus-names 3
Horus 50
   „ with head-dress of Amen . . . 32
   „ Min 50
   „ Ra 50
Horuza 39, 49
Hotep-du-Neit 8
House of Bread 24
Hyaena 8
Hypocephali bronze 38, 49, 50

Implements, flint . . . 7, 8, 10, 11, 12, 16, 25
Ink drawing 31
   „   „ on vases 4
Inlaid glass eyes 38
Inlay, ribbed 25
   „ jasper head from 31

Inscribed objects of foundation deposits . . . 30
    ,,   cylinder jars of King Ka 3, 4
Inscriptions, earliest known 3, 4
Iron in foundation deposits 32
Ivory arrow-head 24
   ,,   bracelet 5
   ,,   draughtsman 24
   ,,   inlay 24
   ,,   pin 24
Jasper girdle tie 39
   ,,   head 31
   ,,   in foundation deposits 32

Ka=Ap 3
Ka 4, 5
   ,,   inscriptions of 3
   ,,   tomb of 3
Ka 44, 45
   ,,   emblem 29
   ,,   name, inversion of 3, 4
   ,,   of Osiris 44
Keeper of the cattle in Rameses' temple . . 31, 45
Keni-Amen 45
Kha-kau-ra 1
Kha-sekhemui, bowl of 4, 5
   ,,   flints of 8
   ,,   figure of Min 4
   ,,   vases of 7
Khay 31
Khemenu 50
Khentamenti 29, 32
   ,,   chantress of . . . 40, 49
   ,,   sistrum-player of . . 48
Khepera 50
Kher-heb 41, 42
Khnum 50
Khnumy, priestess 34
Knives, flint 8, 10, 11, 16
Kom-es-Sultan 9
Koptos, workmen of 1, 2
Kudu (?) on painted pot 23

Lazuli amulets 38
   ,,   bead of Psamtek 25
Lector, or *Kher-heb* 44
Levels in stratified town 10
Limestone bowl 6
   ,,   cup 5
   ,,   figures 26, 33
   ,,   ,,   of Assa . . . 28
   ,,   ,,   of Tahutmes III . . 30

Limestone figures, kneeling 29, 42
   ,,   ,,   ,,   of Hora . . . 31
   ,,   mortar 33
   ,,   sculpture of Nectanebo I . . 33
   ,,   stand of Amenhotep III . . 31
Lintel of Tahutmes II and III 30
Lintel of Tahutmes III 30
List of offerings 30

M. tombs . . . . 14—20
Maa-kheru 31
Mac Iver, D. R. 1, 4
Magic, sympathetic 17
Malachite face-paint 17
Mastabas 34
   ,,   wrongly called pyramids . . 36, 37
Mat-sign *p* 4
Measurements of columns of Antef . . . 28
Mena—Aha 5, 6, 7
   ,,   flints of 8
Menat, or counterpoise, worn by deceased . . 30
Mentu-em-hat 31, 17
Mer, see Superintendent.
Mer-en-ra, blocks of 27, 41
Mer-neit, flints of 8, 12
Mer-se-ka 7
Mer-se-kha 4, 6, 8
Mertiu-heru 35, 36, 48
Mert-tefnut 35, 36, 48
Min, oldest drawn figure of 4
Min-mes, high priest of Anhur . . . 44
Model coffin 35, 36, 48
   ,,   flint knife 24
   ,,   forked lance 24
   ,,   shell of alabaster 30
   ,,   tools of foundation deposits . . 30
Monkeys, green glazed 25
Mortar, limestone 33
Mummies . . . . 36—39

Naqada, Menite tomb 8, 11
Nar-mer 4, 5
Nebta-ahyt 38, 49
Nebui Sma 5
Nectanebo I, sculpture of 33
   ,,   II, temple of 32, 33
Nefertiut, chantress of Khentamenti . . 40, 49
Nefert-uben 29
Neheb-ka 50
Neithotep vase of 5
Nekht, Prince 28, 41, 42

Nekht-hor-heb, cartouche of 33
  ,,   statues of age of 33
Nes-her 35, 48
Netter, bone 18, 24
Numerical signs 4
Nut, representations of . . . 36, 38, 39, 50

Objects in M. tombs 17, 18
Obsidian amulets 38
Offering chambers 34
Offerings, altars of . . . 29, 32, 42, 48
  ,,   list of 30
  ,,   *per-kheru* . . . 44, 48, 51
  ,,   table of 45, 51
Order of pre-Menite Kings 5
Osiride statuettes . . . 35, 36, 38, 39
Osiris, bronze figures of . . . 30, 32, 45
  ,,   high priest of 46
  ,,   *ka* name of 44
  ,,   Khentamenti . . . 29, 45
  ,,   mummified 32
  ,,   shrine of 9
  ,,   temenos of . . . 1, 9, 27
  ,,   temple 9, 27
  ,,   ,,   inscriptions . . 41—48
  ,,   titles of . . . 45, 46, 48, 51
Ox-bones in tomb 17

Pa-asi 44
Paint, white 18
Painted pottery 23
  ,,   ,,   Aegean 6
  ,,   ,,   ,,   date confirmed . . 6
  ,,   sculpture 30
Palettes, slate . . . 17, 23, 24, 25
Panelling 3, 4
Papyrus 36, 38
Paraffin wax, for preserving wood and cartonnage . 38
Pe, shrine of Buto 41
Pectoral 38, 40
Pediment of breccia 34
Pedu-asar 39
Pedu-en-ast 39, 49
Pendants 23
Perabsen 4, 6
Per-kheru offerings . . . 42, 44, 48, 51
Pesh-ken amulet 24
  ,,   ,,   connections of . . 24
Pilgrim bottle 6, 34
Pillared court 34
  ,,   hall 29

Pin-ivory 24
Plans of tombs 15
Plaques of foundation deposits . . . 31, 32, 33
Porphyry 21
  ,,   amulets 38
Portrait-head of Aahmes I 30
  ,,   ,,   Amenhotep I . . . 30
  ,,   ,,   in granite . . . 28
  ,,   ,,   in quartzite . . . 32
  ,,   sphinx of Tahutmes III . . 30
Position of bodies in M. graves . . . 15, 16
Pot-marks 23
Pottery 12, 13, 14, 18
  ,,   Aegean 6
  ,,   Black incised . . . 5, 24
  ,,   Black-topped . . . 6
  ,,   dating of 6
  ,,   discs 24
  ,,   figures 26
  ,,   fire-rings 25
  ,,   hand-made 6
  ,,   kine 26
  ,,   of foundation deposits . . 30
  ,,   painted 6
  ,,   styles in various reigns . . 6, 13
  ,,   wavy-handled . . . 6, 35
Prehistoric burials 34, 35
Pre-Menite kings . . . . . 3—5
  ,,   ,,   order of . . . 5
Priest, high, of Amen 47
  ,,   ,,   Anhur . . . 44, 47
  ,,   ,,   Hathor . . . 49
  ,,   ,,   Isis and Min . . 47
  ,,   ,,   Mut . . . 49
  ,,   ,,   Osiris . . 46, 47
  ,,   ,,   Un (?) . . . 49
  ,,   of Amen Ra . . . 47
  ,,   ,,   Hathor and Uazit . . 39
  ,,   ,,   Shu and Anhur . . 44
  ,,   ,,   Sokar . . . 31
  ,,   *hesi-ka* . . . 48, 49, 51
  ,,   *sem* 46
  ,,   *uab* 42
Psamtek 33
  ,,   bead of 25
Ptah-em-ua, statue of . . . 29, 31, 45
Publication of results 1, 2
Pylon, granite 9, 27
Pyramidion of granite 32
Pyramids, so-called, of Abydos . . 36, 37

Qa, inscription of 5

Qa, gold of 6
   ,, stele of 6
Qema, sign 3
Qemat of Amen 45
   ,,   ,, Isis 44
   ,,   ,, of Khentamenti . . . 40, 49
   ,,   ,, Osiris 44
Quartz, glazed 25
Queen of Zer, hair of 5
Qufti workmen 1, 2

Ra 44, 48
Ra-aa-Kheper-en (Tahutmes II) . . . 30, 48
Ra-Harmakhis 45
Ra-Kha-seshes-Nefer-hotep 29
Ra-Kheper-Ka 42
Ram 50
   ,, god 50
Ra-men-Kheper (Tahutmes III) 44
Ramessu I *ka* name 31
   ,,   II *ankh* of 25
   ,,   ,, cartouche 31, 45
   ,,   ,, gateway of 29
Ra-nub-Kheper (Antef V) 41
Ra-sekhem 29
Ra-sekhem-nefer-hotep 29
Recesses 33
Reed-sign, *a* 4
Res sign 3
Resin, cake of 33
Ribbed glazed tiles 25
Ring, gold 34
Ring stands 14
Ro, position of 4, 5
   ,, sealing of 4
   ,, tomb of 5
Ro sign 4
Roofing of tombs 15, 37
Royal tombs, flints from 8
   ,,   ,, objects from 7, 8
   ,,   ,, pottery from . . . 3, 4, 6
Rush mat 16

Salt, packets of 39
Sandstone figure 29
Sarcophagi . . . . 34—40
Saws, flint 12
Scarab and wings 39, 40
Scrapers, flint 7, 8, 11
Scribe 43, 48
   ,, of accounts 51

Scribe, royal 44, 45, 49
Sealing of Ro 4
   ,,   ,, Shepses-Kaf 27
Sealings 24
   ,, material of 5
Sebekhotep III. 9
   ,,   ,, inscription of 29, 42
   ,, and Nefertuben 29, 42
Sed festival of Amenhotep II 30
Sekhet, bronze figure of 32
Sem priest 46
Semer-uati 41, 51
Sen sign 7
Senb, scribe 43
Sequence dates, prehistoric 22
   ,, of Pre-Menites 5
Serpent, pottery 25
Sesh sign 4
Shell, notched 24
Shells, string of 24
Shepses, *ka* name of Shepses-kaf . . . 27
Sickles, *see* Flint saws.
Silver pilgrim bottle 34
   ,, in foundation deposit 32
Sit-Hathor 39, 43
Sit-Pepy 29, 43
Skulls of animals in graves . . . 16, 17, 18
Slate palettes for face-paint . . 17, 23, 24, 25
Sma 5
   ,, vases of 5, 7
Snaa-ab 43
Snaring nets 23
Sokar 45
   ,, sanctuary of 45, 46
Sphinx of Tahutmes III 30
Spindle whorls 24
   ,,   ,, dating of 25
Standard-bearer of Amen 45
Statues 31, 33, 46
Statuette 44
Statuettes, Osiride 35, 36, 38, 39
Steatite amulets 38
   ,, beads 16
   ,, head 31
Stele of Ameny and Sit-Pepy 29, 43
   ,, ,, Auhet-abu 29, 31
   ,, ,, Khay and Ymamu 31
   ,, ,, Narmer 8
   ,, ,, Nekht 28, 41
   ,, ,, Qa 6
Steles 7, 8, 27, 29, 43, 44, 45, 51
Stone grinders 25, 26

Stone, vases, *see* Vases.
Stones in M. graves 16
Stratified town 10
  ,,   ,, flints of . . . . 10—12
  ,,   ,, levels of 10
  ,,   ,, pottery of . . . . 12—15
Superintendent of cattle 31, 45
  ,,   ,, granary . . . 45, 47
  ,,   ,, palace 43
  ,,   ,, temple 41
  ,,   ,, treasury . . . 43
  ,,   ,, *zazanut* . . . 46
Suten-Ap 3
Suten du hotep formula . . 42, 43, 45, 48, 49, 51
Suten ka ankh 29
Suten-khaker 41, 42, 43
  ,,   ,, in connection with *uartu* . . 42
Suten sign 3, 4
  ,, connection with *qema* . . . 3
Syenite cup 5, 7
Sympathetic magic 17

Ta-se-nekht 35, 36, 48
Table of offerings 45, 51
Taharqa, Vizier of 31
Tahutmes II and III reigning together . . 30
  ,,   ,, ,, ,, lintel of . . 30, 43
  ,, coffin of 35, 48
Tahutmes III 9, 30
  ,,   ,, foundation deposits . 30, 32
Temenos of Osiris 1, 9, 27
  ,, excavation of . . . 9, 10
  ,, plan of 9
  ,, tombs in 14
  ,, wall 27
Temple of Anhur 41
  ,, Osiris 27
  ,,   ,, age of . . 1, 9, 27
  ,,   ,, columns of . . 28
  ,,   ,, halls of . . . 29
  ,,   ,, rebuildings of . 9, 31
  ,,   ,, statues of . . 28, 29
  ,,   ,, steles of . . 27—29
  ,, Rameses . . . 31, 45
Thiy Nefertari 31, 46
Thompson, Herbert 41
Throne-name derived from *ka*-name . . 28
Tiles, ribbed 25
Tomb pits 34
Tombs (M.) early dynastic . . . 14, 15
  ,,   ,,   ,, objects in . 15, 18

Tombs (M.), roofing of 15, 36, 37
  ,,   ,, in relation to town levels . 19
  ,,   ,, ,, ,, kings' tombs . 20
Tools, copper 7, 15, 23, 30
Torso of pottery figure 26
Town site, of early dynasties 10
  ,, levels 10
  ,,   ,, in relation to sequence dates . . 22
  ,,   ,, ,, ,, ,, kings' tombs . . 21
  ,,   ,, ,, ,, ,, M. tombs. . . 19
Trained workmen 1, 2
Tray, alabaster 7
  ,, wooden 7, 37
Trial-piece 31
Triangular pot 14
Tum 45
Two-finger amulet 39

Uab-priest 42, 51
Uah-ab-ra 35, 48
Uartu of the prince's table . . 29, 42, 43
  ,, in connection with *suten khaker* . . 42
Undisturbed burials 18
Un-nefer 31, 44, 46
  ,,   ,, granite statue . . . 31
  ,,   ,, and wife, granite group . . 31, 44
Up ast 7
Up-uat 29, 42
Ur-maau, scribe 45
Usertesen I 9
  ,,   ,, slab of . . . 28, 42
  ,,   ,, basement of slab of . . 29
  ,, III 1
Ushabti boxes 38, 39
Ushabtiu 38, 39, 40
  ,, dating of 38, 39
  ,, fixed number of . . . 38, 39
Uza-eye 39, 50
Uza-headed goddess 50

Variants of names 35
Vase grinders . . . . . 12, 25—6
Vases of stone 12, 16, 18, 20
  ,, cylinder 19, 22, 23
  ,, handled 12
Vulture and uraeus 32, 48

Wartw of the prince's table . . 29, 42, 43
Wax, paraffin, for preserving wood and cartonnage . 38
Weigall, A. E. 2, 7, 27
  ,, ,, ,, on inscriptions . . . 41—46

Weight	. . . .	25
White paint	. . . .	18
Wooden framing in tombs.	. . . .	16
„ tray	. . . .	7, 37
Workmen, Qufti	. . . . . .	1, 2
„ trained	. . . .	2
Ymamu	. . . .	31
Zazanut, mer	. . . .	46

Zed	. . . .	35
Zed-her	. . . .	35, 37, 38
Zer	. . . .	6
„ flints of	. . . .	8
Zeser	. . . .	5
Zeser-ka-ra	. . . .	43
Zet	. . . .	8
„ flints of	. . . .	6, 37
Zigzag pattern on bird's leg bone	. . . .	7
„ „ „ Aegean pottery	. . . .	6

F.P.

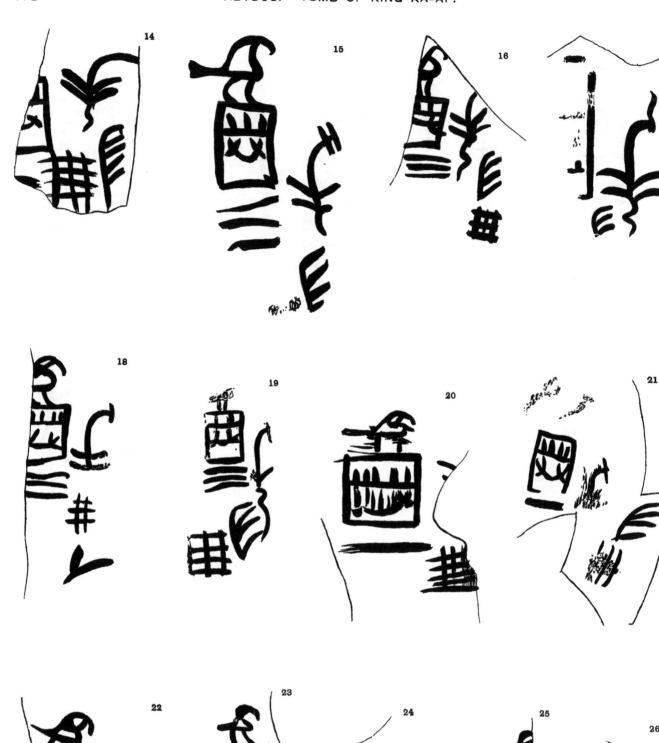

F. P.

FP.

1.   VASES OF SMA.   2.   3. BRACELET OF BENERAB.   4. KHASEKHEMUI.   5. VASE OF ZER.

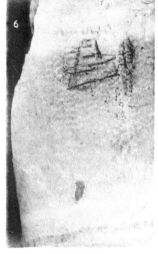 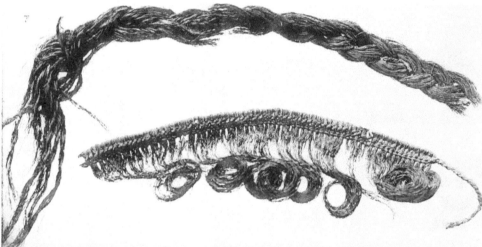

6. VASE OF NEITHOTEP.   7. 1:1 PLAIT AND FALSE FRINGE, TOMB OF ZER.

  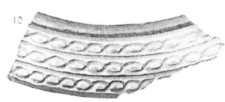

10. BOWL EDGE OF ZER.

8. VASE OF ZER.

9. POTTERY FROM ZER.

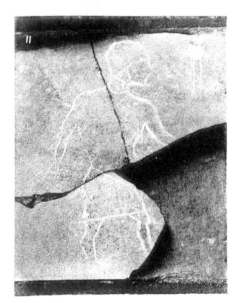  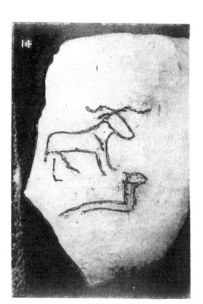

11. DWARF OF ZER.   12, 13. IVORIES OF ZET.   14. VASE OF W.

1 : 2   ALABASTER OF AZAB.
See R.T. i, vi. 2, vii. 10, viii. 11.

4 : 3   VOLCANIC ASH OF QA.

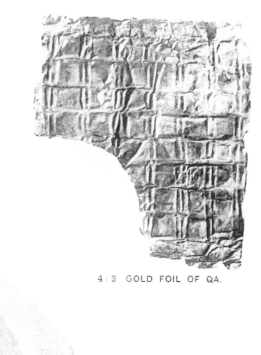

4 : 3   GOLD FOIL OF QA.

1 : 4   QUARTZOSE STELE OF QA.

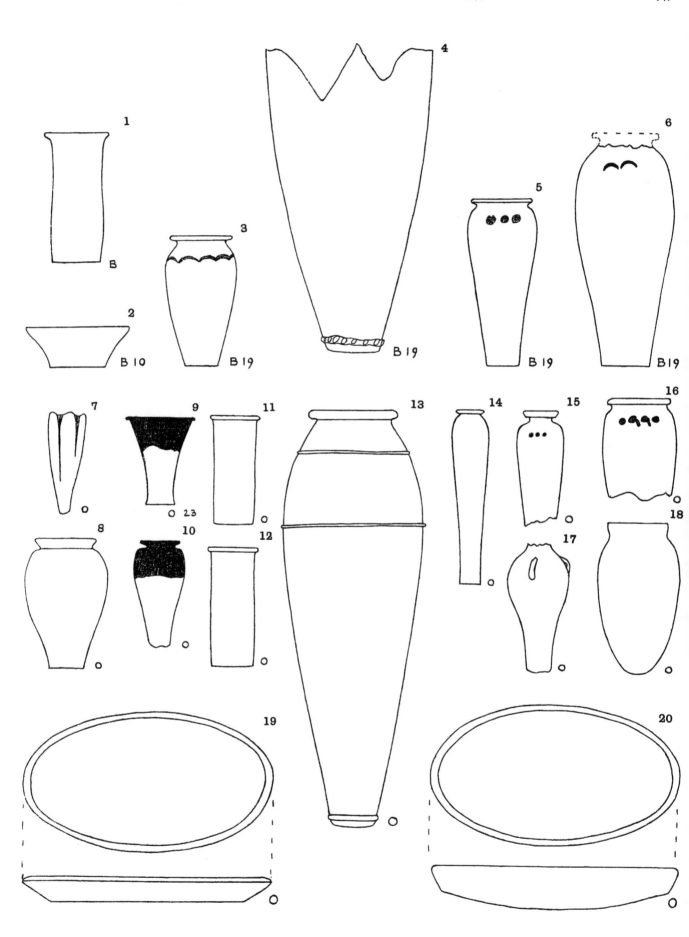

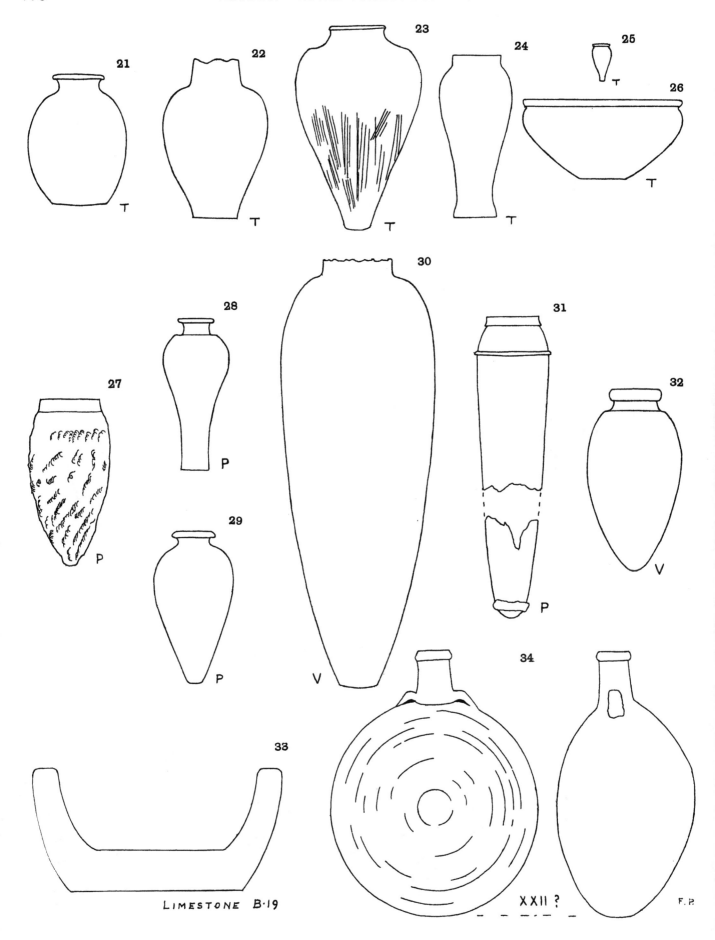

LIMESTONE B·19

XXII ?

F. P.

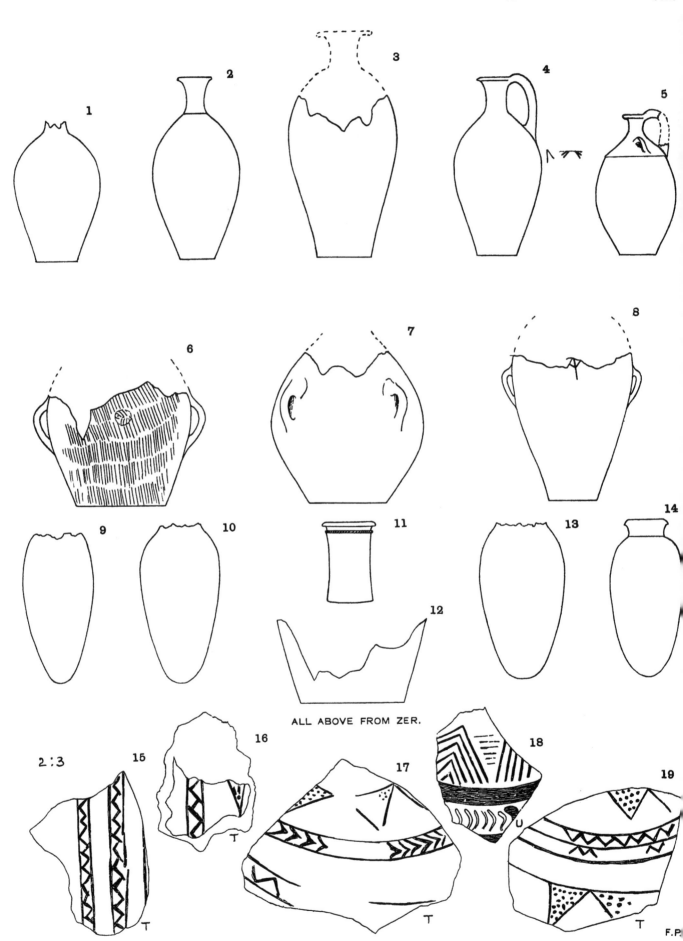

ALL ABOVE FROM ZER.

2:3

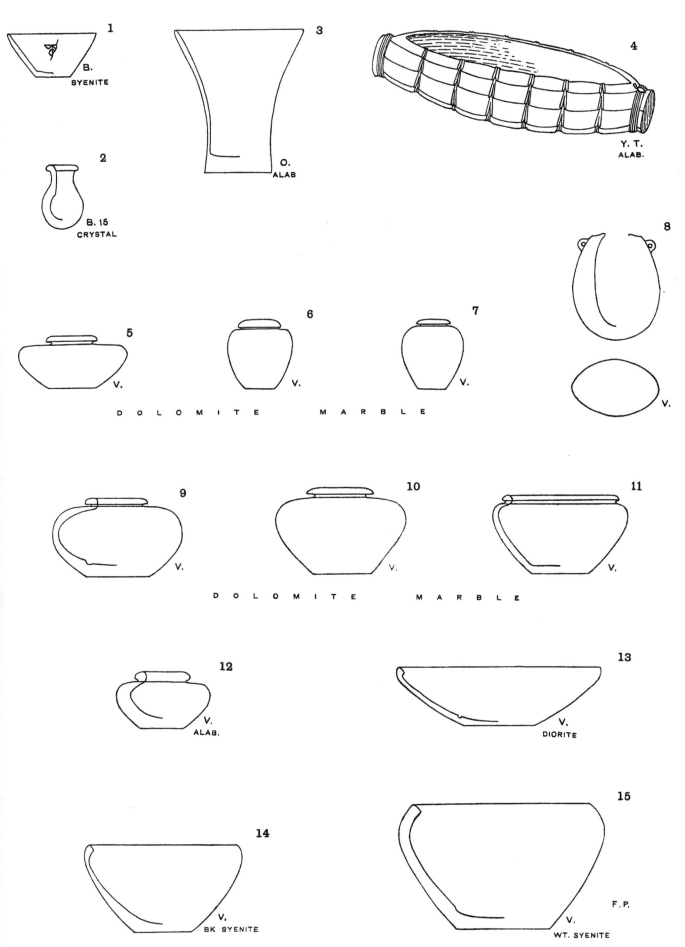

1
B.
SYENITE

2
B. 15
CRYSTAL

3
O.
ALAB

4
Y. T.
ALAB.

5
V.

6
V.

7
V.

8
V.

D O L O M I T E   M A R B L E

9
V.

10
V.

11
V.

D O L O M I T E   M A R B L E

12
V.
ALAB.

13
V.
DIORITE

14
V.
BK SYENITE

15
F.P.
V.
WT. SYENITE

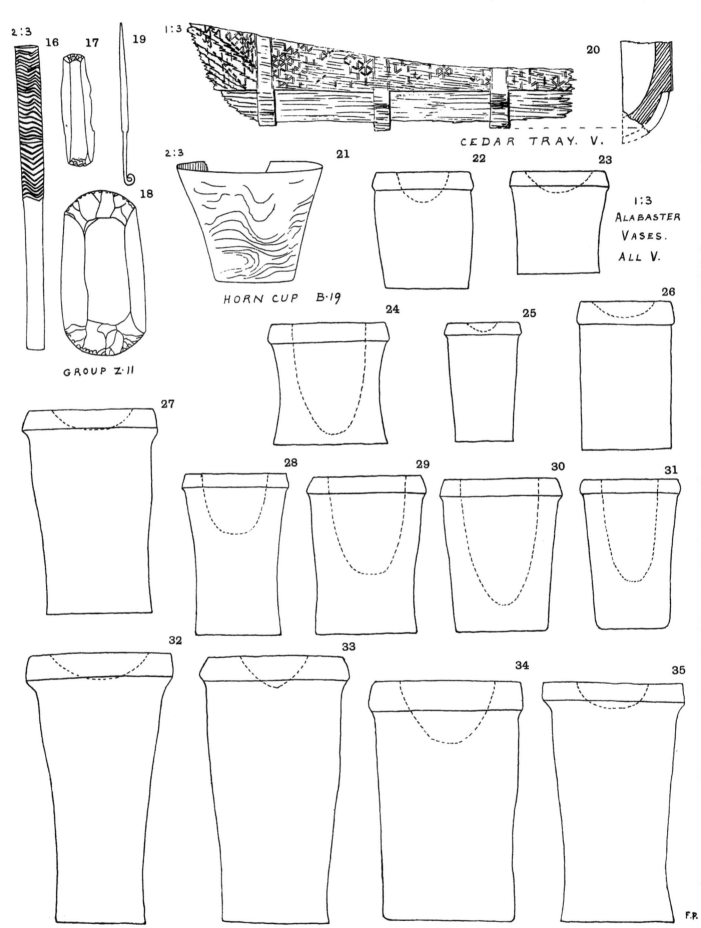

2:3

16   17   19

18

GROUP Z·11

1:3

20

CEDAR TRAY. V.

2:3   21   22   23

HORN CUP B·19

1:3
ALABASTER
VASES.
ALL V.

24   25   26

27

28   29   30   31

32   33   34   35

F.P.

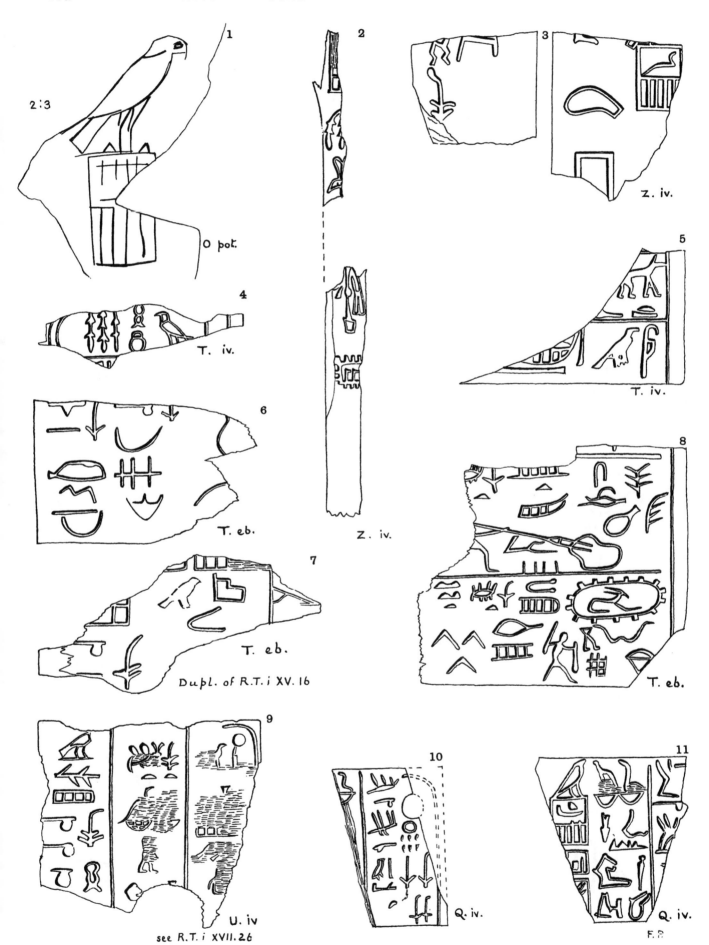

2:3

1

O pot.

2

3

Z. iv.

4

T. iv.

5

T. iv.

6

T. eb.

7

T. eb.

Dupl. of R.T. i XV. 16

Z. iv.

8

T. eb.

9

U. iv

see R.T. i XVII. 26

10

Q. iv.

11

Q. iv.

F.P.

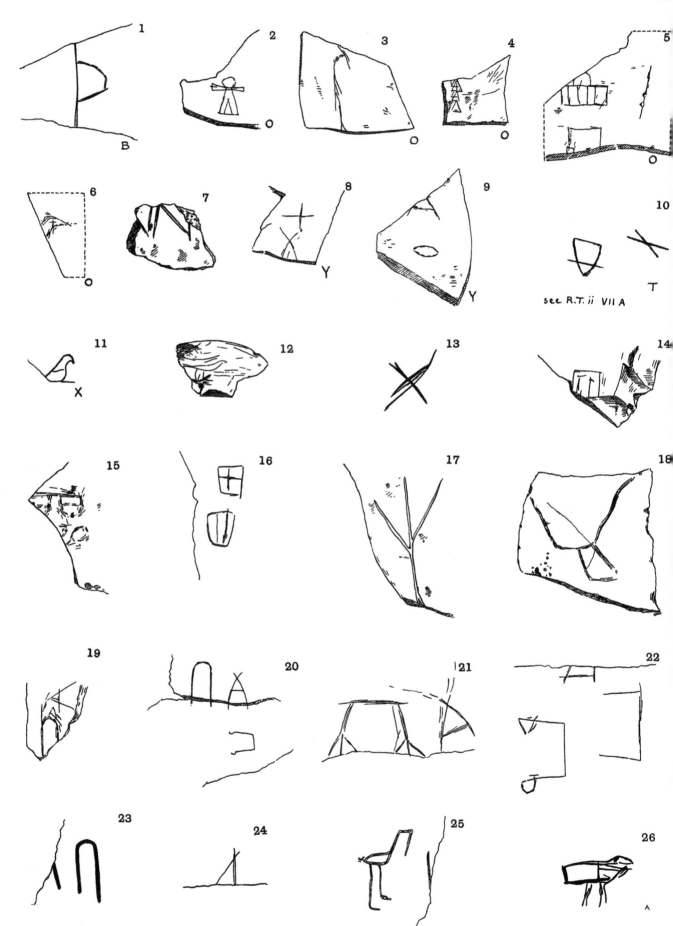

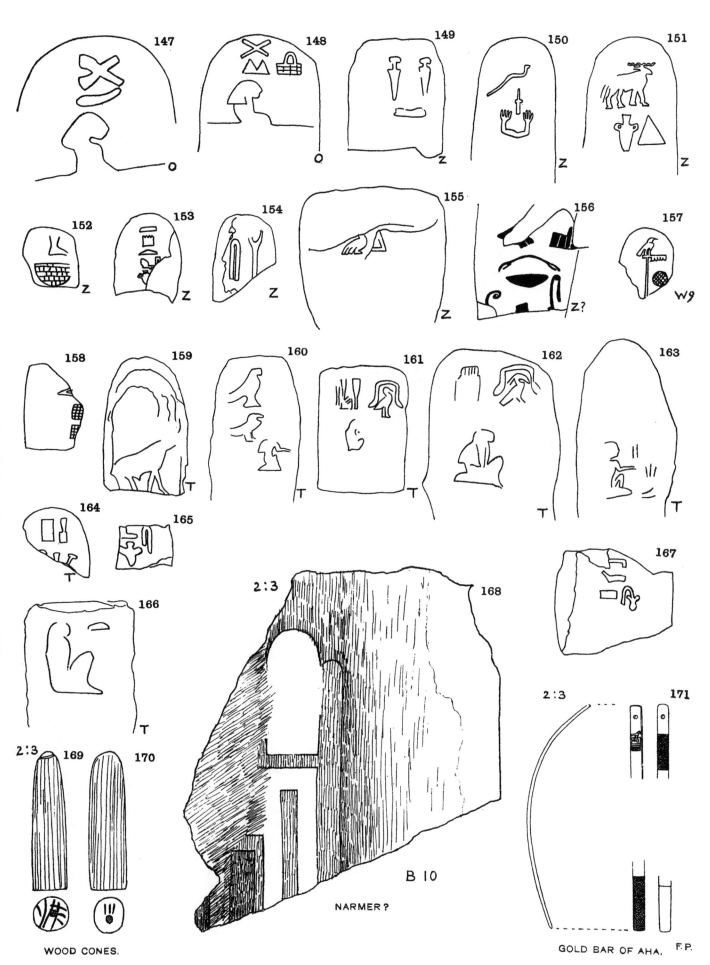

WOOD CONES.

2:3

B 10

NARMER ?

GOLD BAR OF AHA.   F.P.

MENA. ZER. ZET. MERNEIT. DEN.

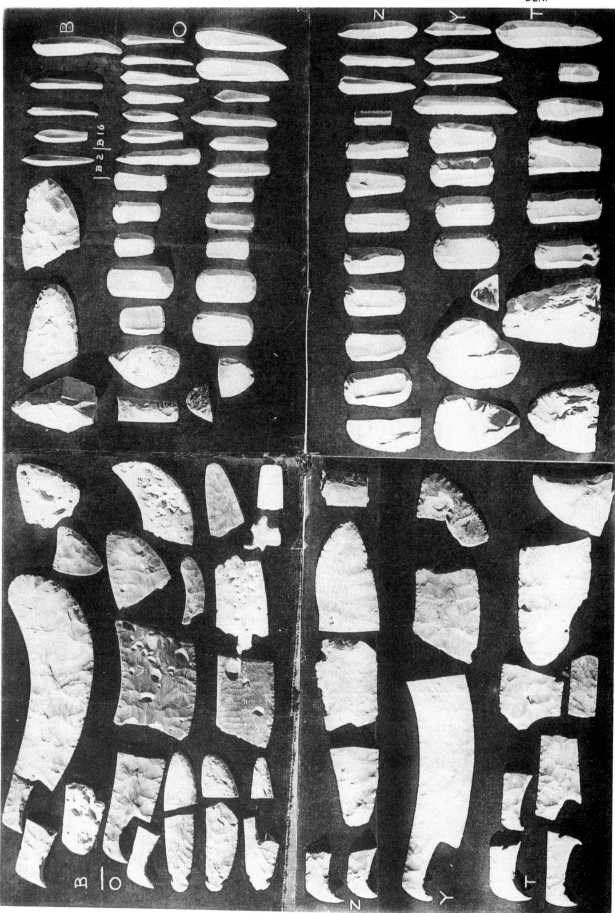

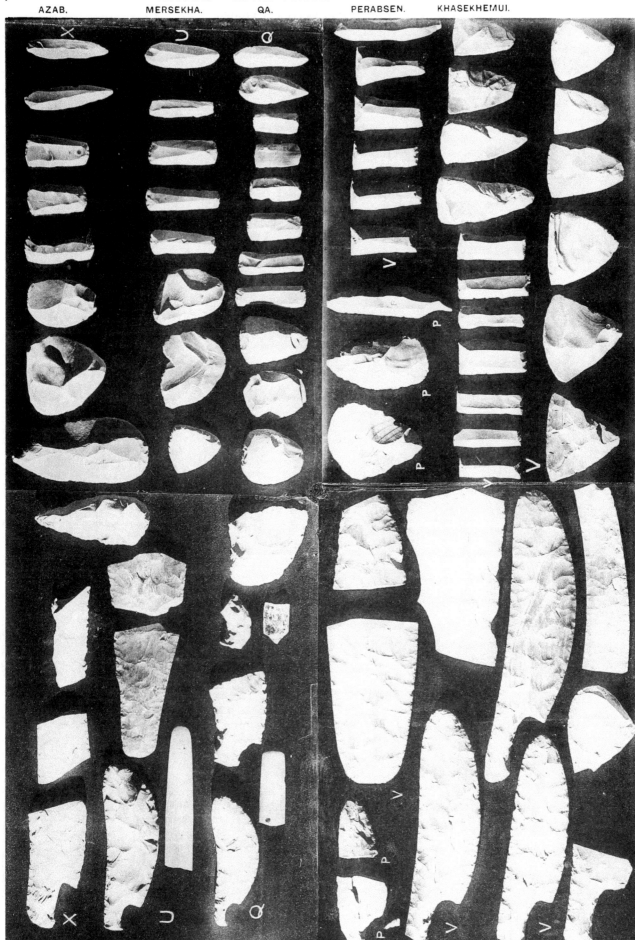

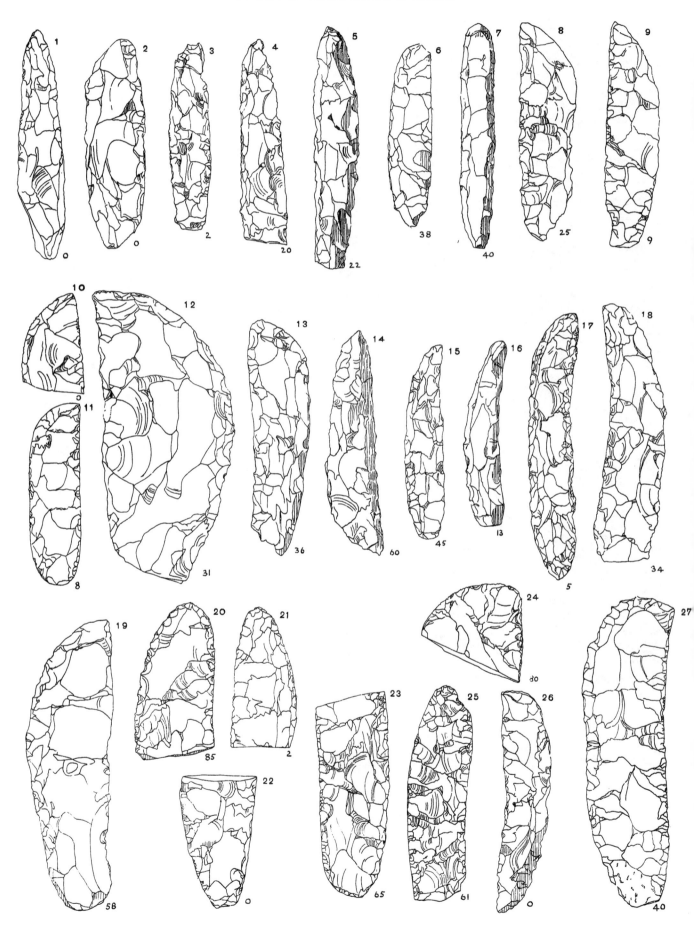

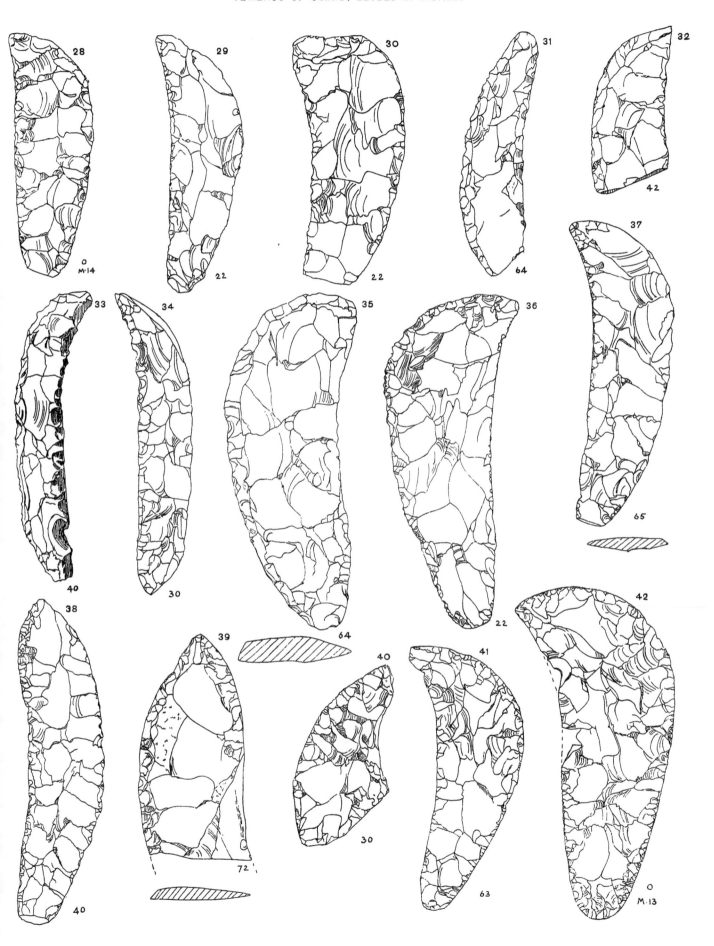

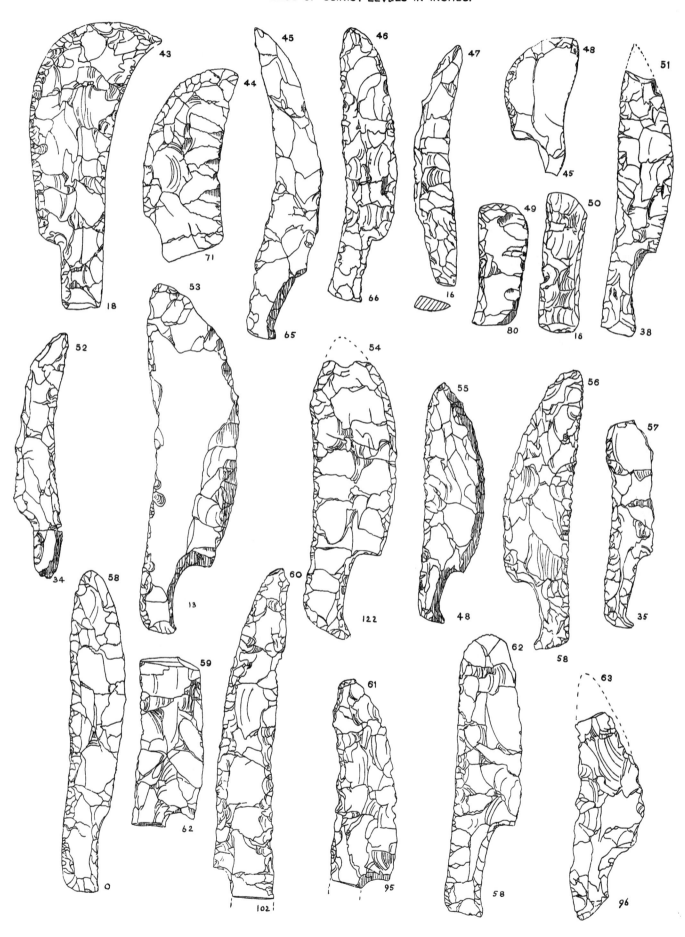

TEMENOS OF OSIRIS: LEVELS IN INCHES.

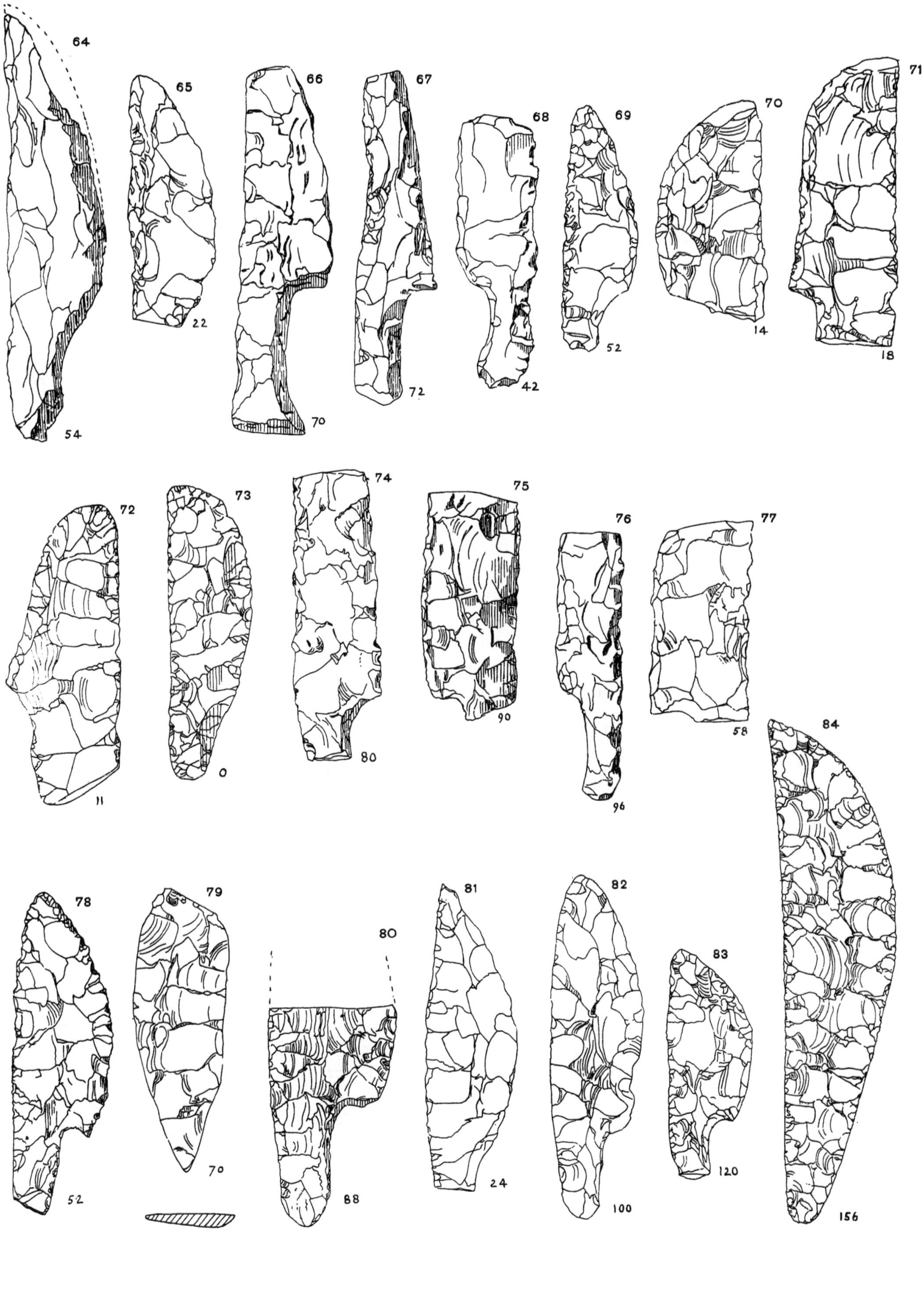

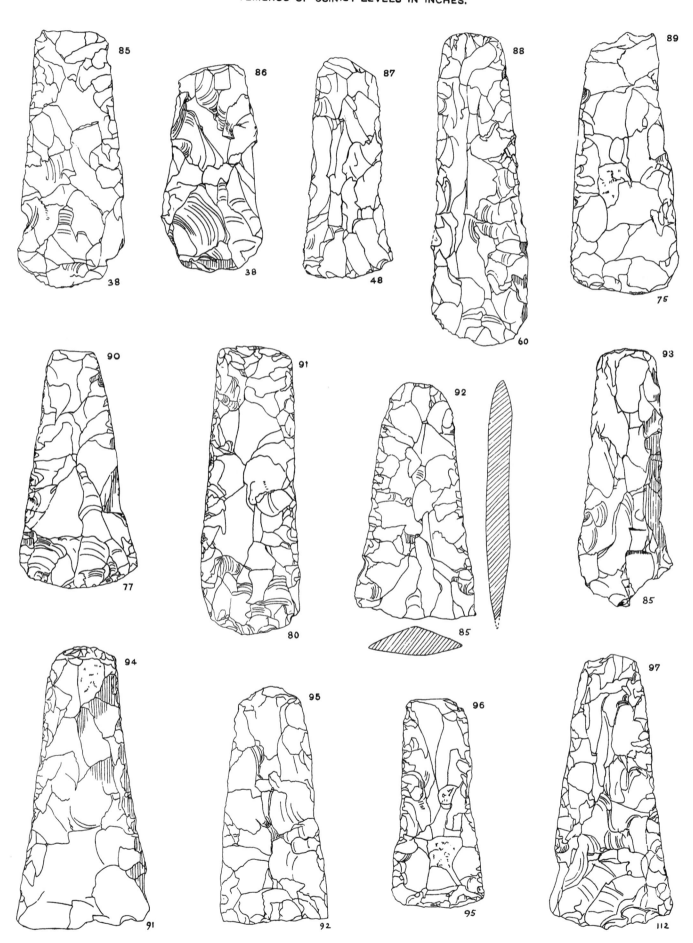

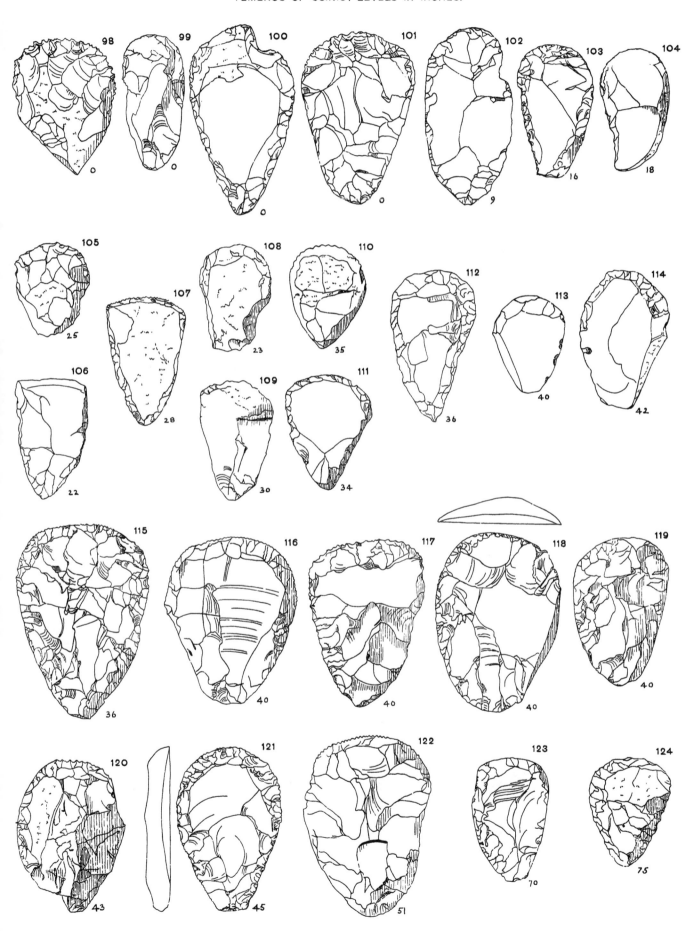

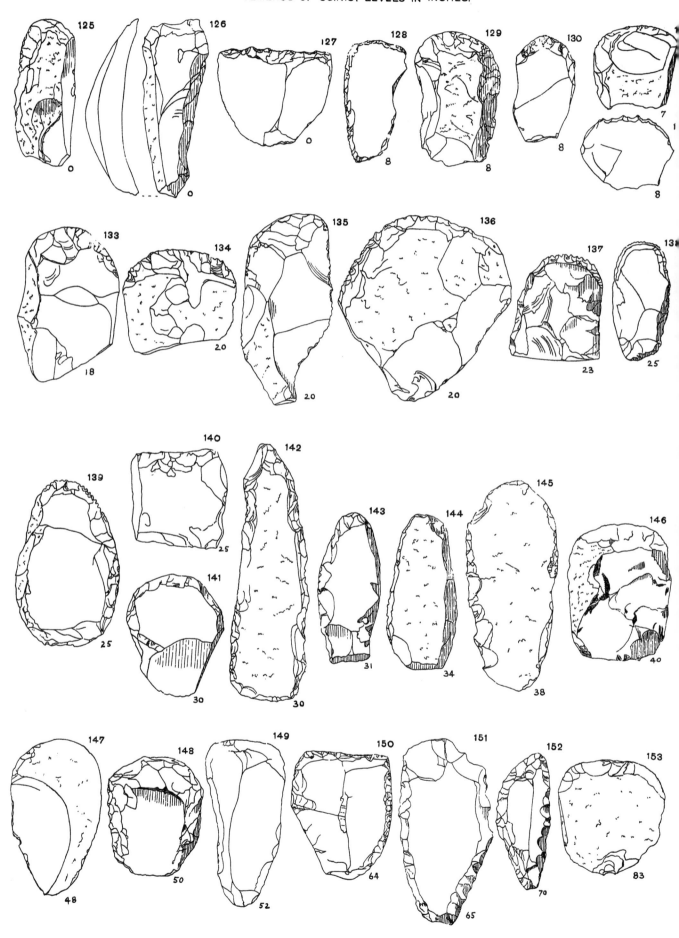

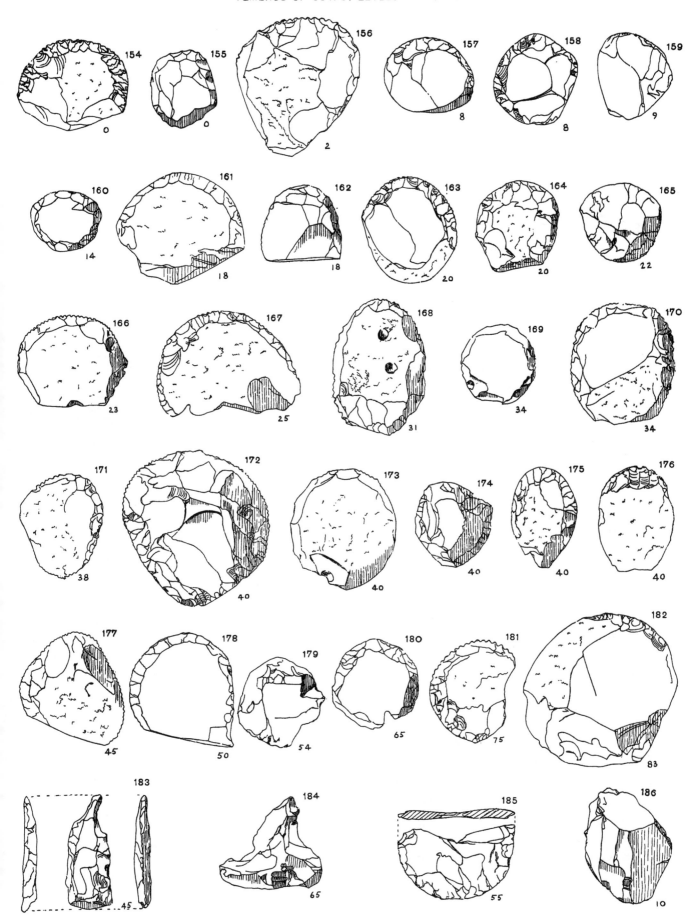

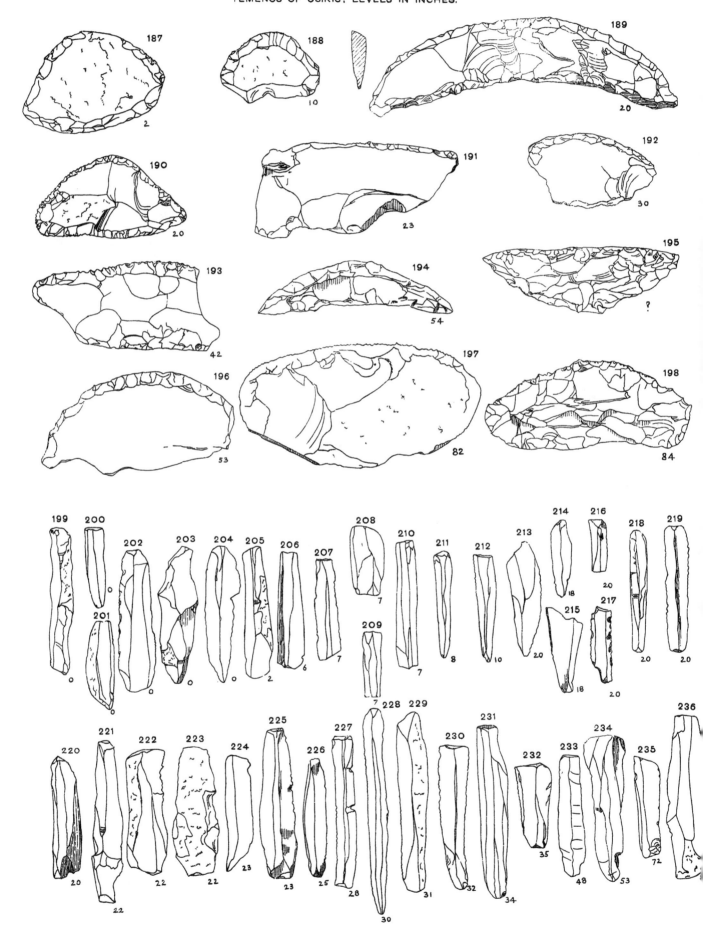

1 : 2 ABYDOS. FLINT FLAKES, TIPPED, WORKED, ROUNDED, SQUARE. XXV.

TEMENOS OF OSIRIS: LEVELS IN INCHES.

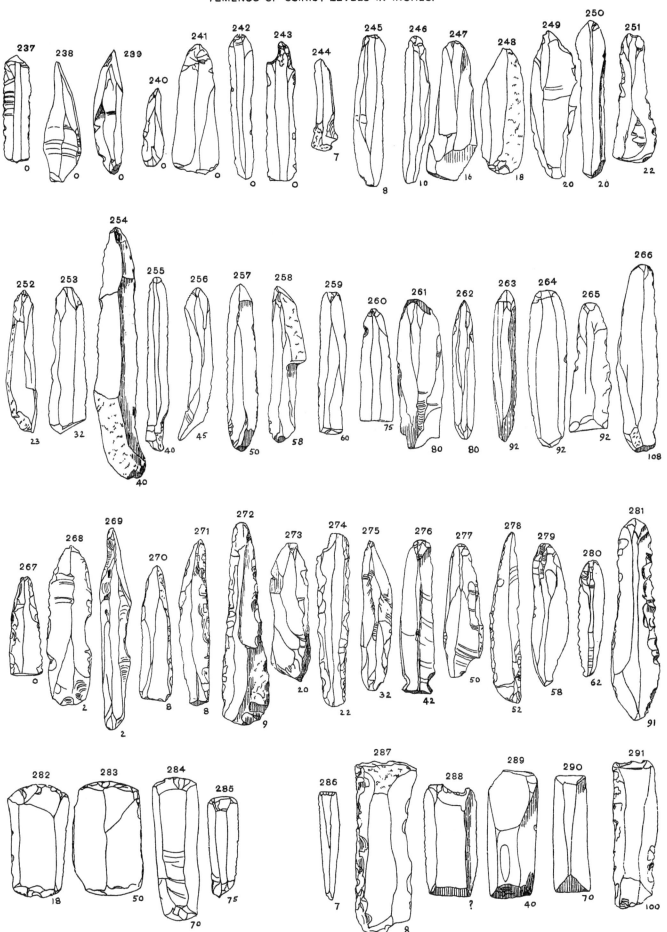

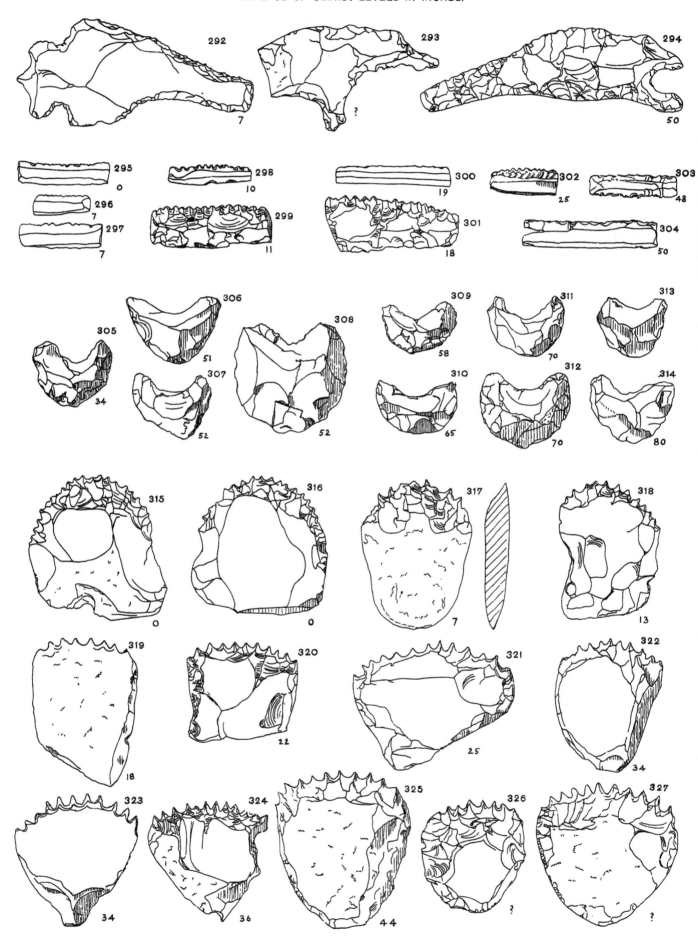

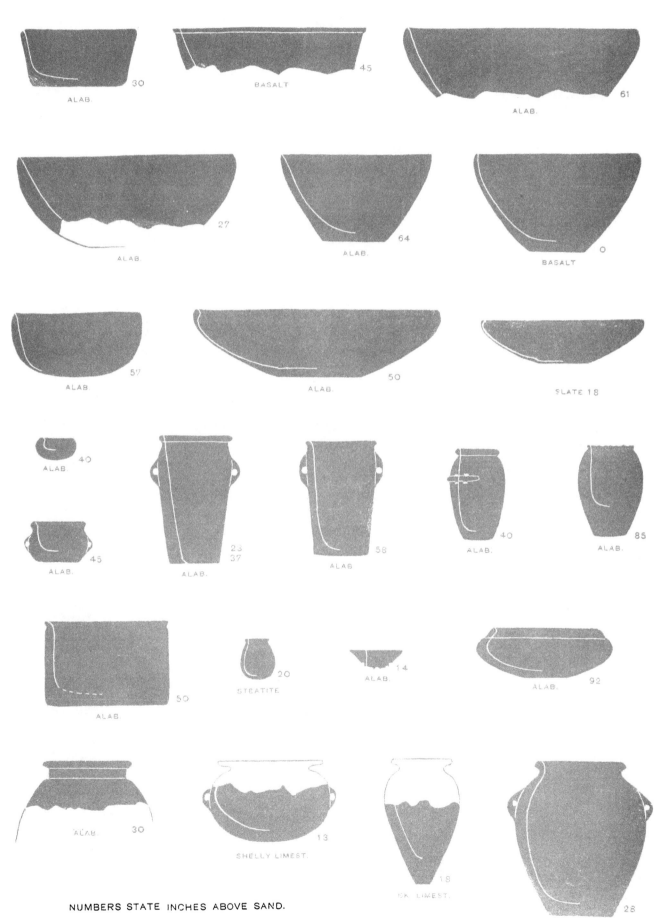

NUMBERS STATE INCHES ABOVE SAND.

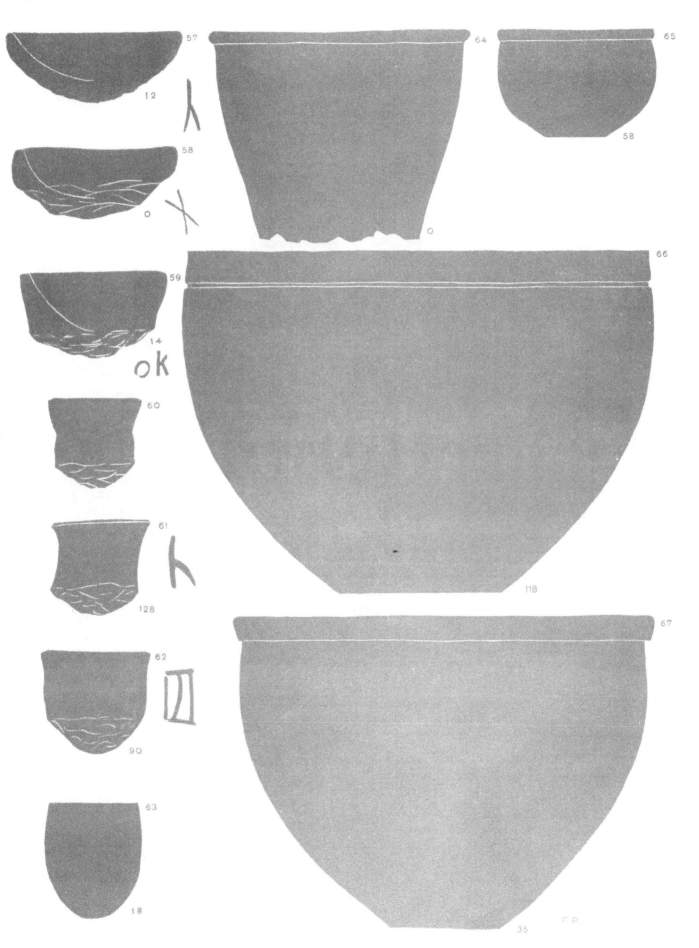

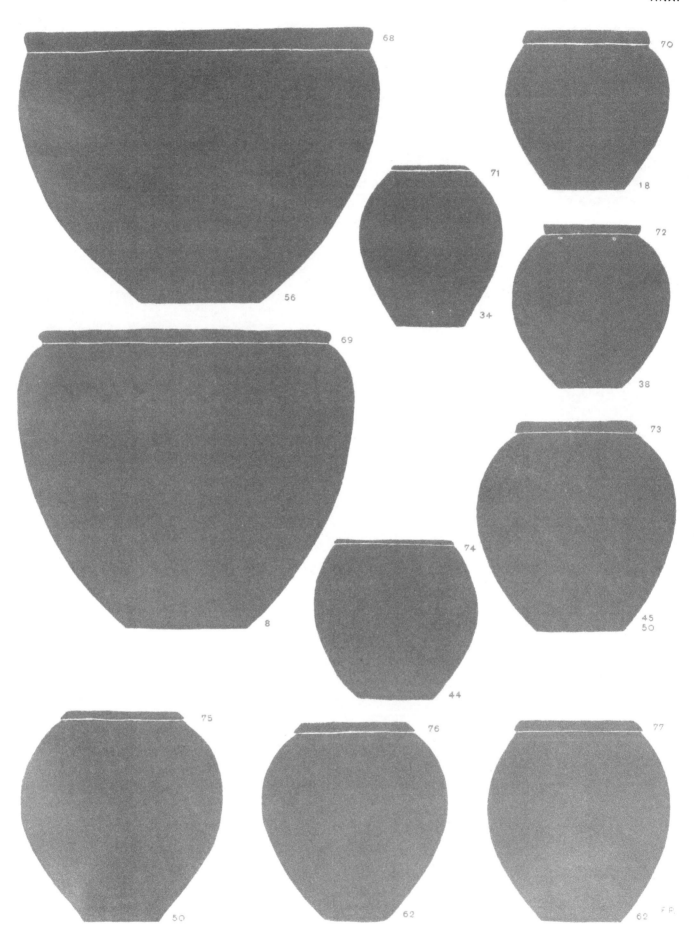

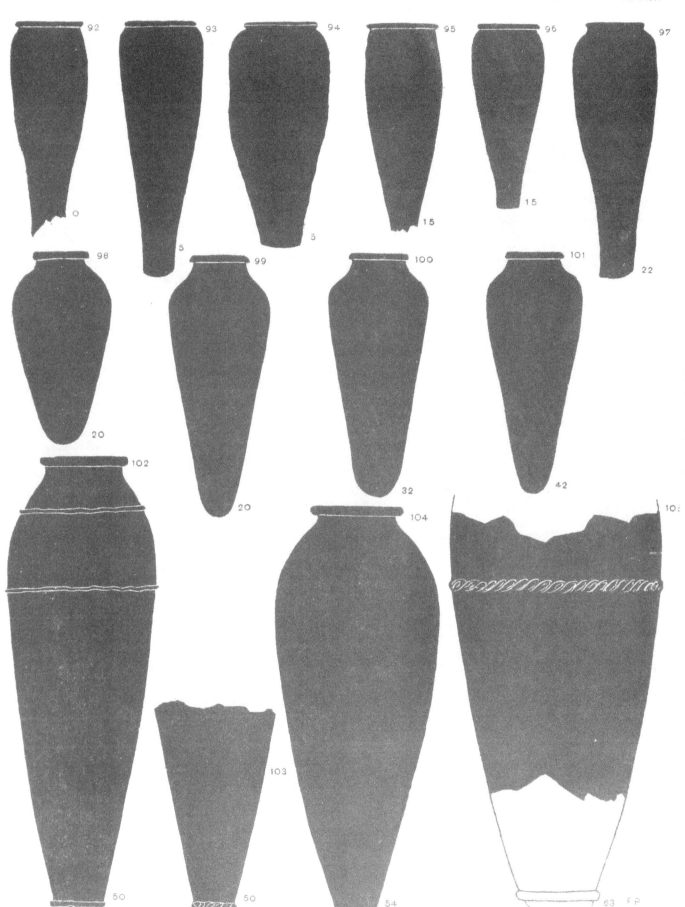

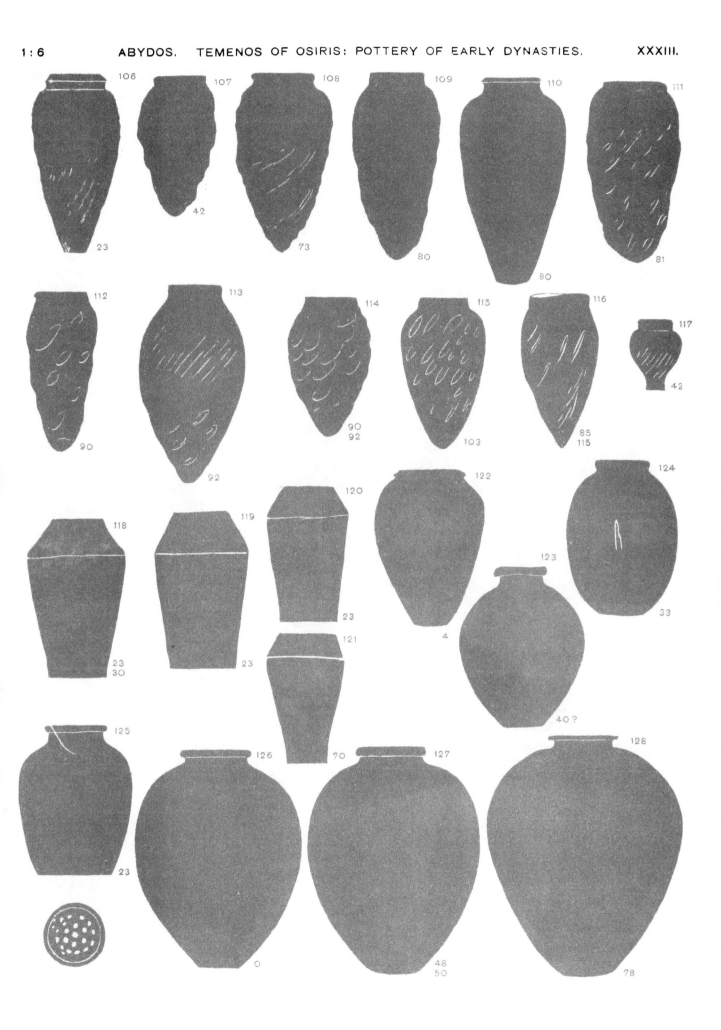

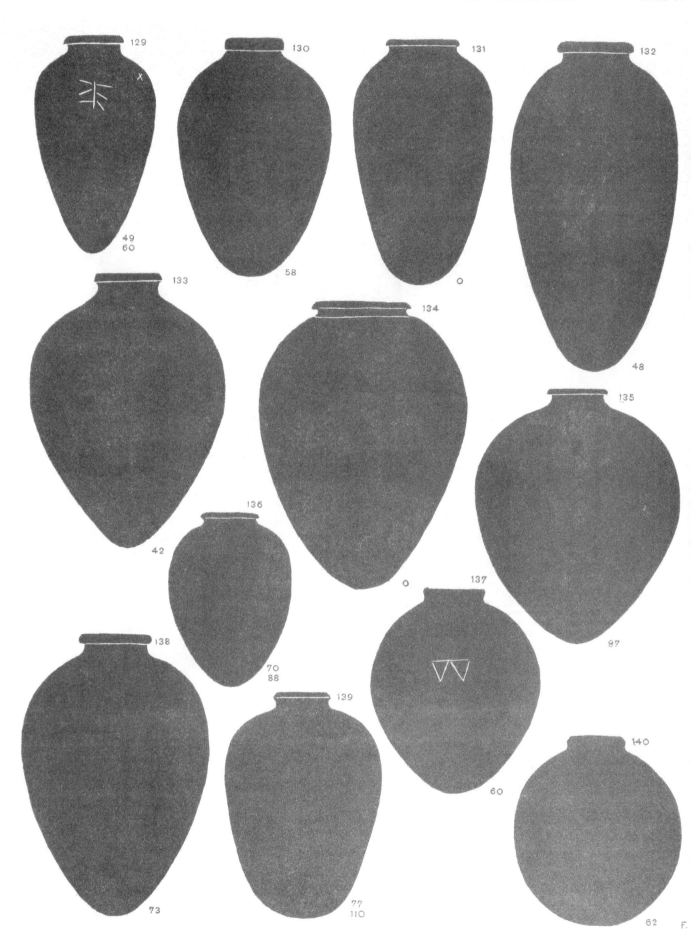

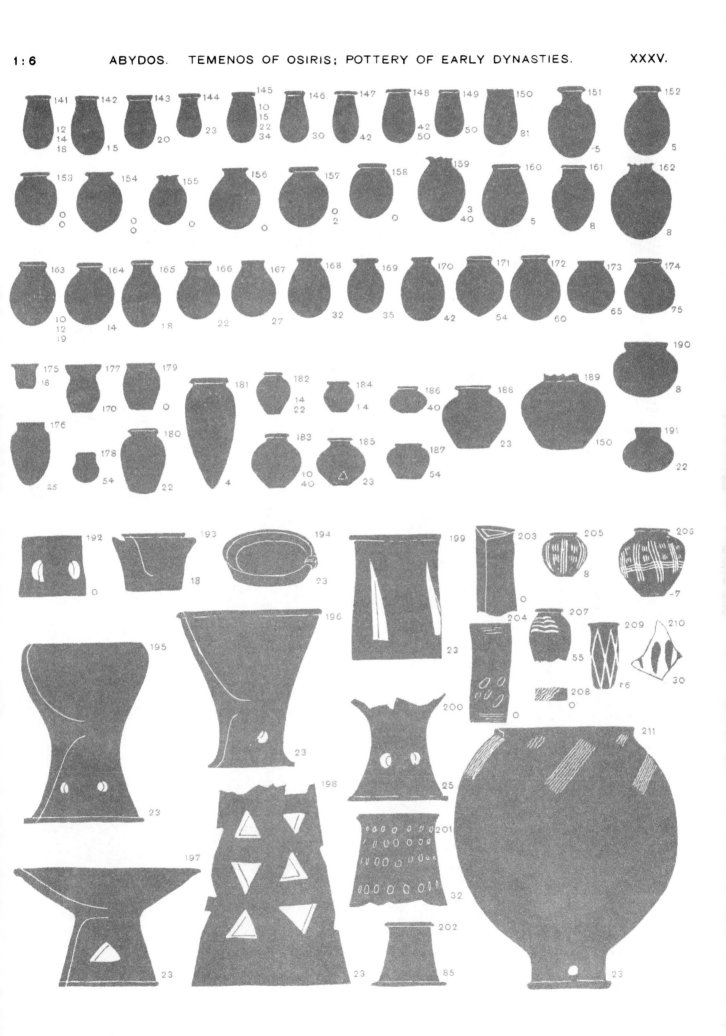

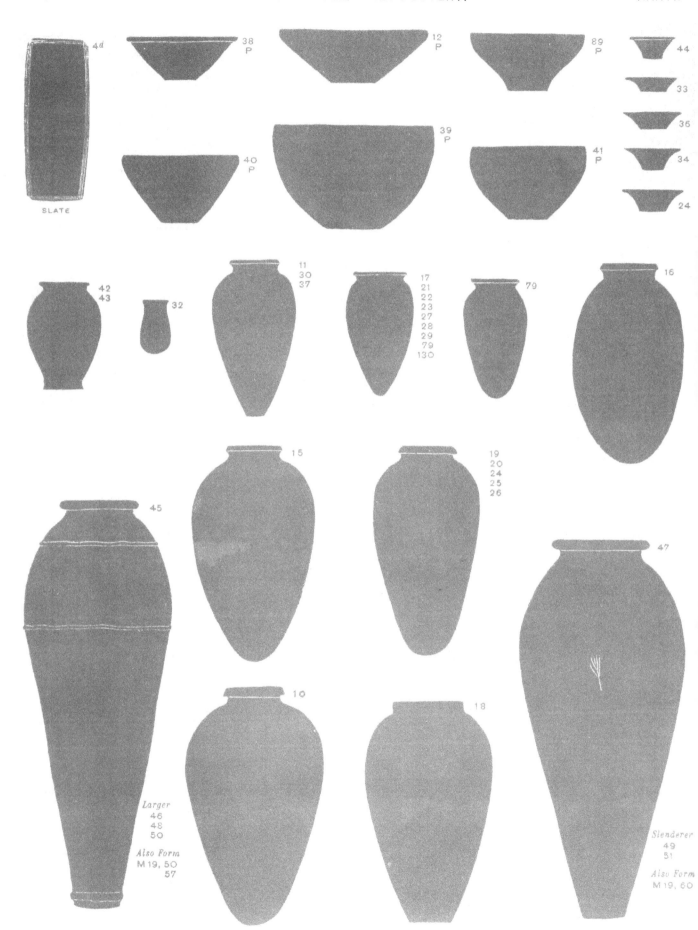

SLATE

4 d

38 P

12 P

89 P

44

33

36

40 P

39 P

41 P

34

24

42 43

32

11 30 37

17 21 22 23 27 28 29 79 130

79

16

45

15

19 20 24 25 26

Larger 46 48 50

Also Form M 19, 50 57

10

18

47

Slenderer 49 51

Also Form M 19, 60

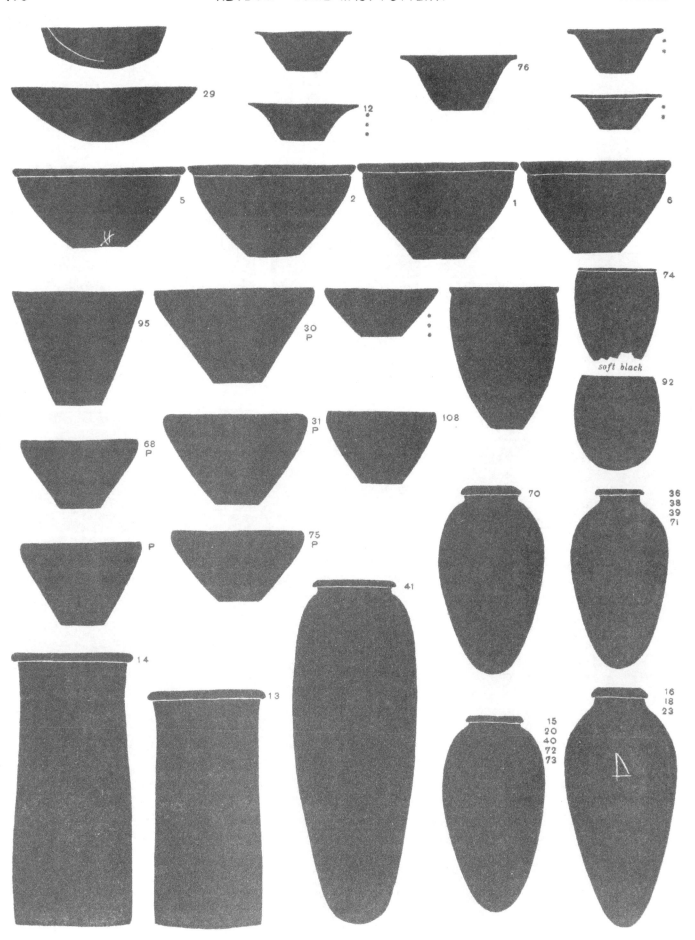

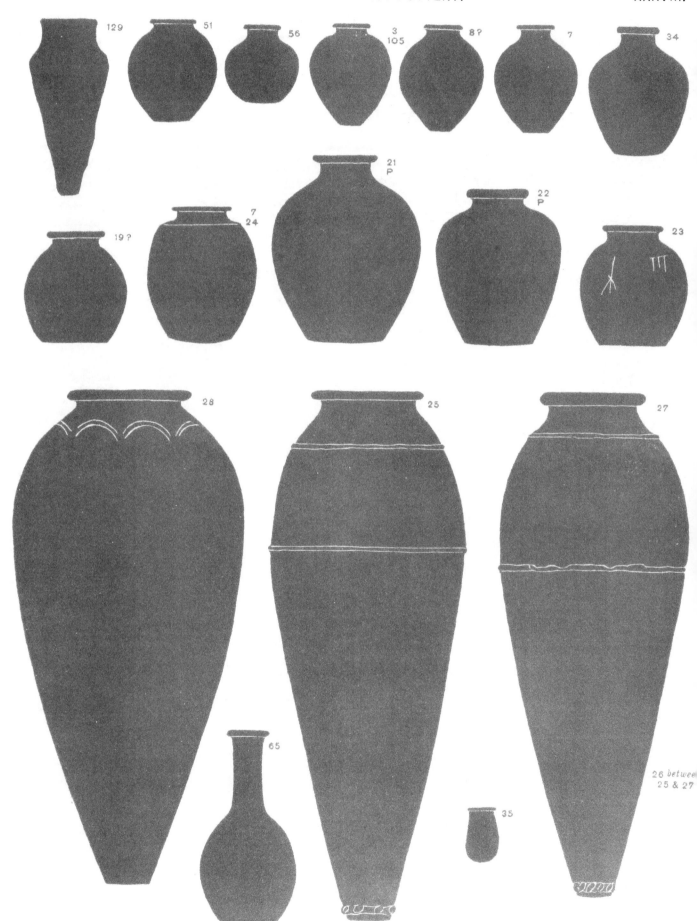

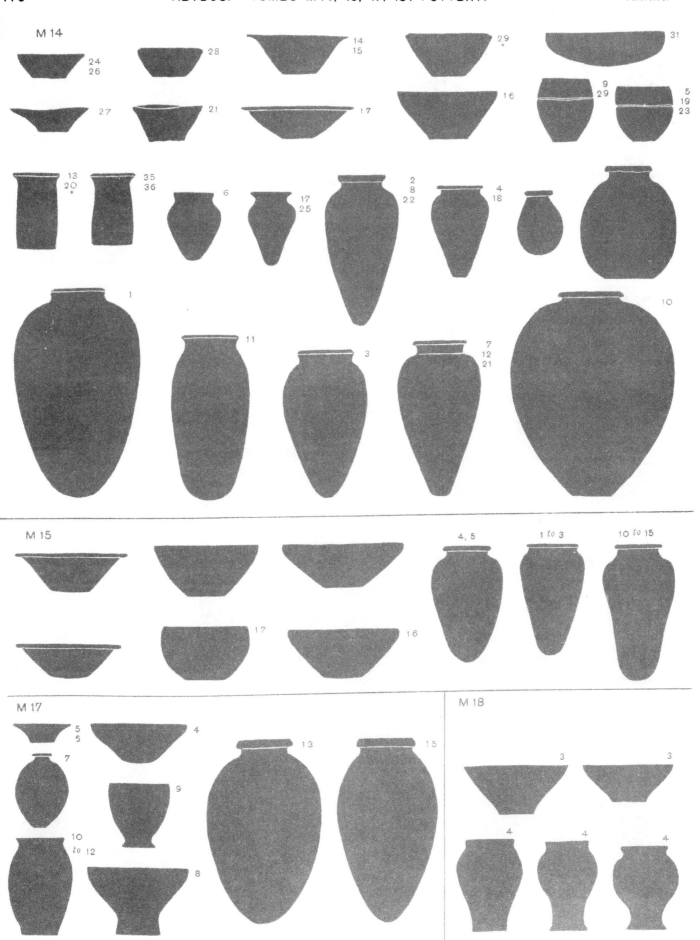

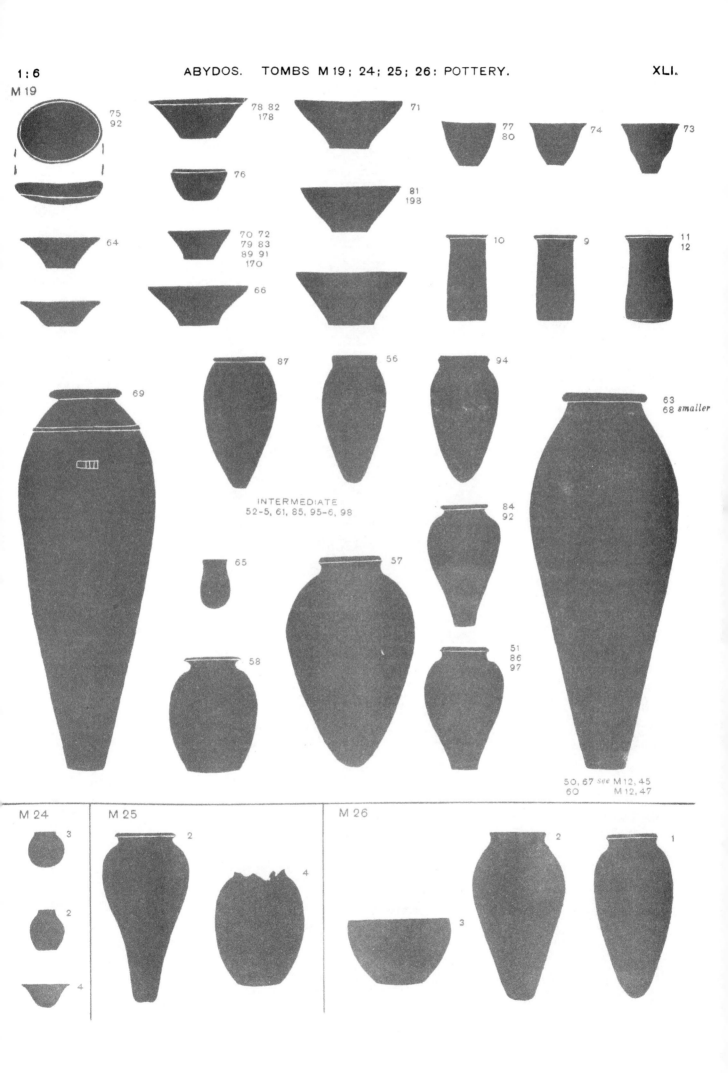

M 19

75
92

78 82
178

71

77
80

74

73

76

81
198

64

70 72
79 83
89 91
170

10

9

11
12

66

87

56

94

63
68 *smaller*

69

INTERMEDIATE
52-5, 61, 85, 95-6, 98

84
92

65

57

51
86
97

58

50, 67 *see* M 12, 45
60   M 12, 47

M 24

3

M 25

2

4

M 26

2

1

2

3

2

4

4

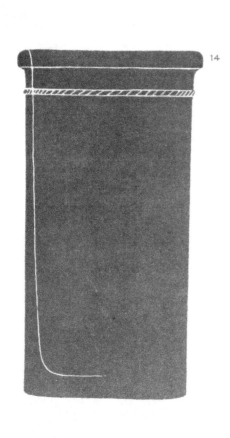

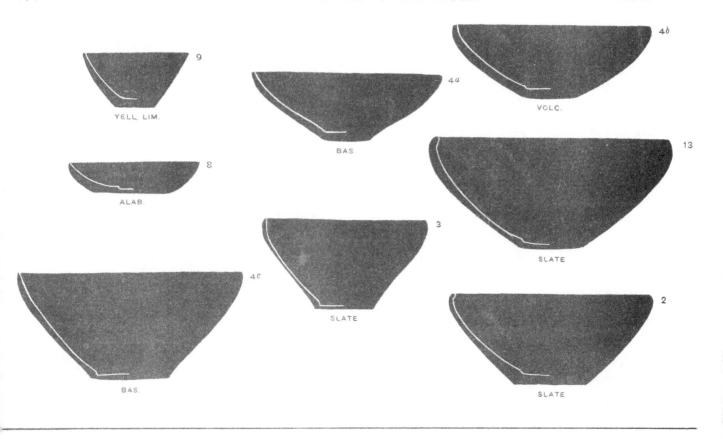

TOMB M 13.

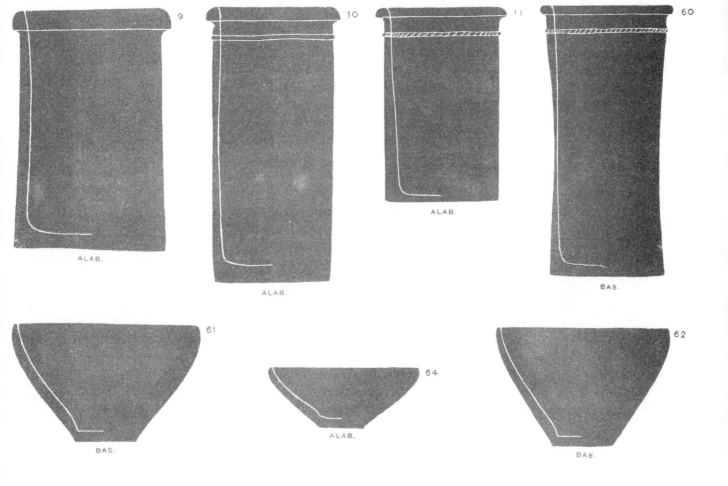

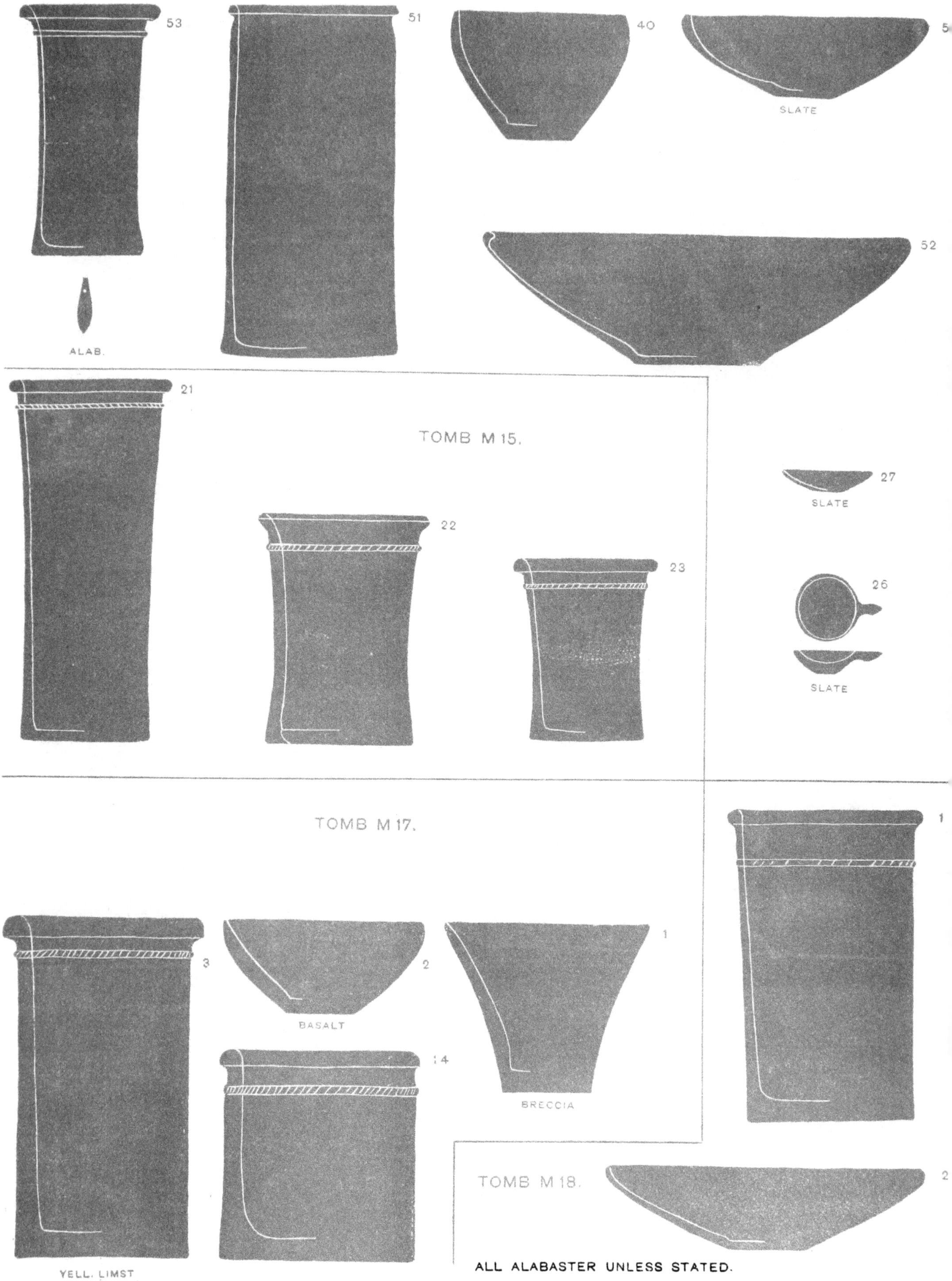

53

ALAB.

51

40

SLATE

52

TOMB M 15.

21

22

23

27

SLATE

26

SLATE

TOMB M 17.

1

3

2

BASALT

1

:4

BRECCIA

YELL. LIMST

TOMB M 18.

2

ALL ALABASTER UNLESS STATED.

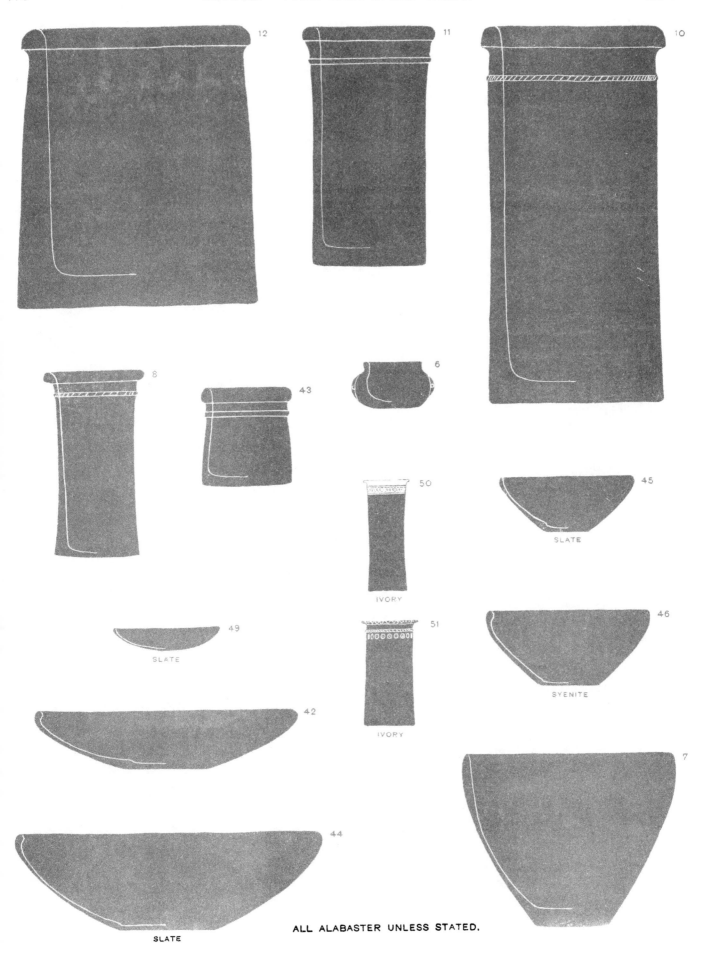

ALL ALABASTER UNLESS STATED.

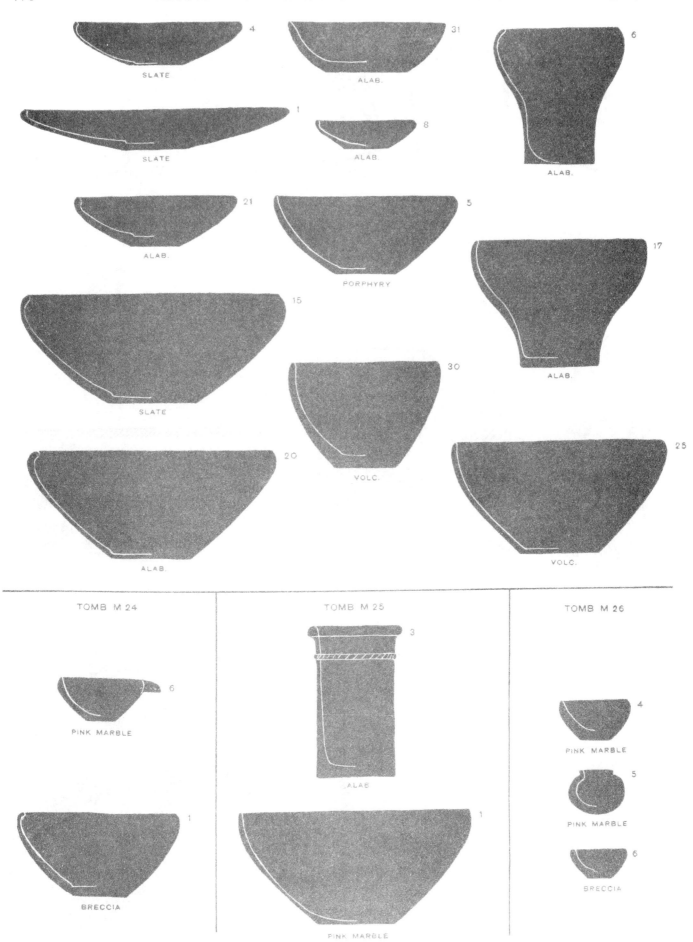

SLATE

ALAB.

ALAB.

SLATE

ALAB.

ALAB.

PORPHYRY

ALAB.

SLATE

VOLC.

ALAB.

VOLC.

TOMB M 24

TOMB M 25

TOMB M 26

PINK MARBLE

ALAB.

PINK MARBLE

PINK MARBLE

BRECCIA

PINK MARBLE

BRECCIA

M 24

M 26

M 25

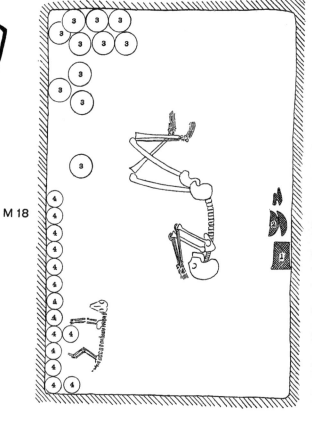

M 18

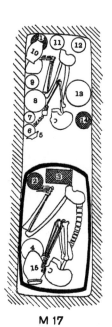

M 17

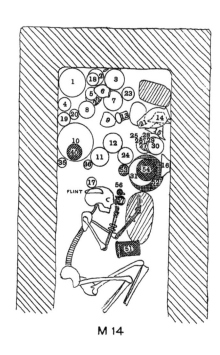

M 14

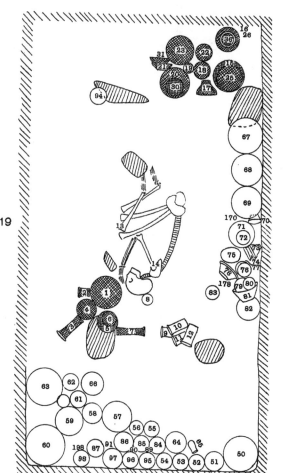

M 19

M 15

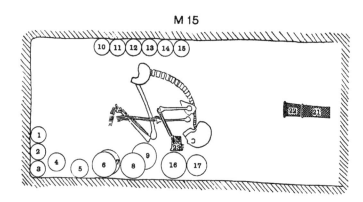

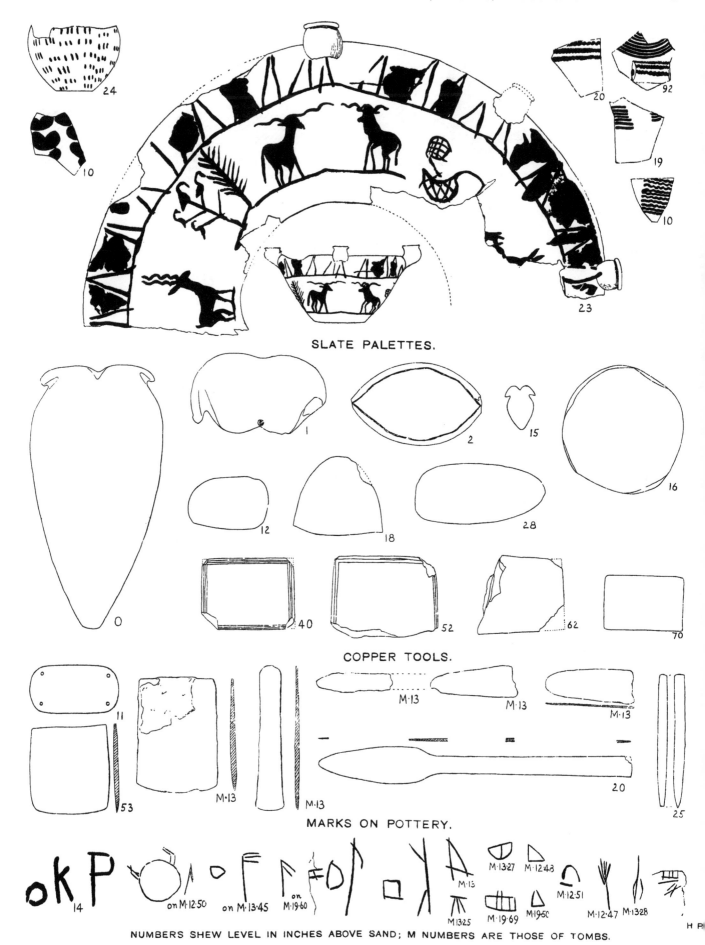

SLATE PALETTES.

COPPER TOOLS.

MARKS ON POTTERY.

NUMBERS SHEW LEVEL IN INCHES ABOVE SAND; M NUMBERS ARE THOSE OF TOMBS.

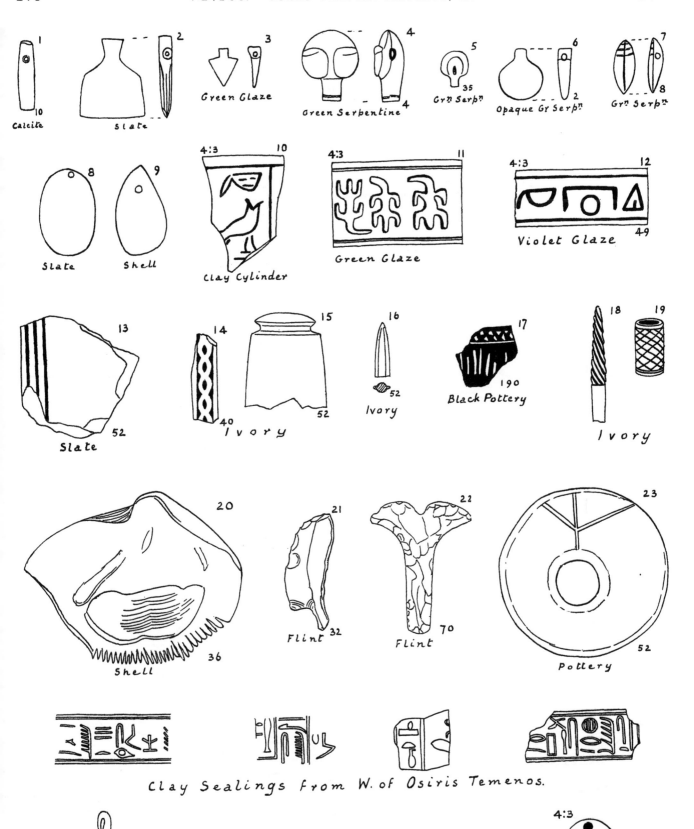

Clay Sealings from W. of Osiris Temenos.

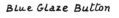

F.P.

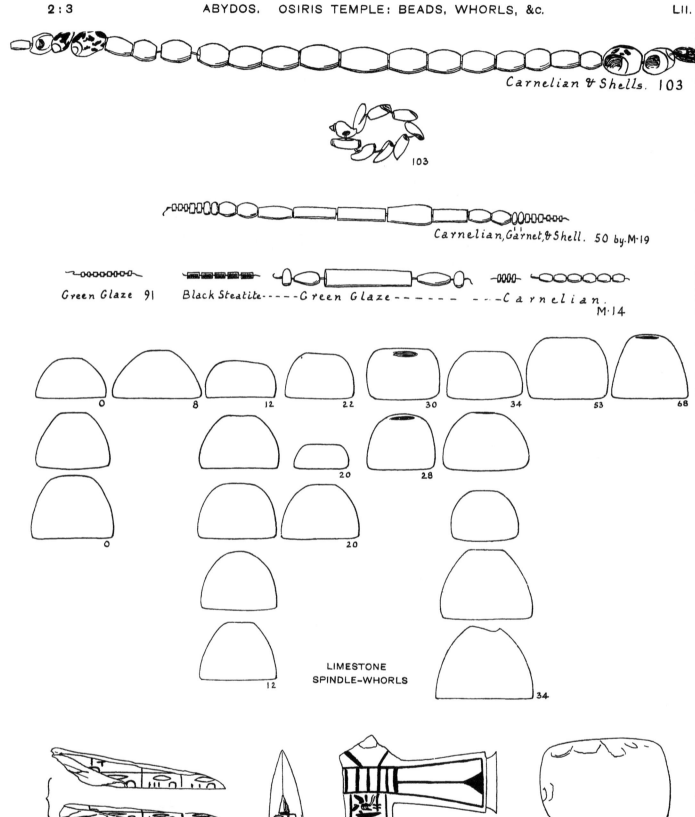

Carnelian & Shells. 103

103

Carnelian, Garnet, & Shell. 50 by. M·19

Green Glaze 91   Black Steatite - - - - -Green Glaze- - - - - - - - -Carnelian.
M·14

0   8   12   22   30   34   53   68

20   28

0   20

LIMESTONE
SPINDLE-WHORLS

12   34

Blue Glaze.

4:3

Lazuli Bead

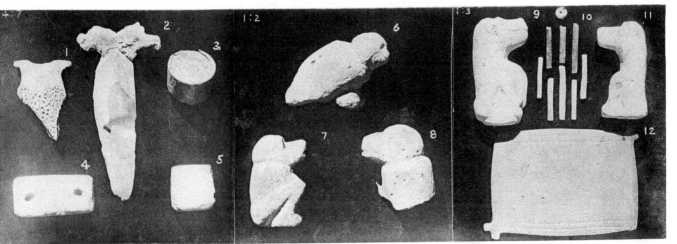

1. BONE.   2. FLINT.   3. GOLD CAP.   4, 5. QUARTZ.   6. LIMESTONE.   7-11. GREEN GLAZE.   12. SLATE.

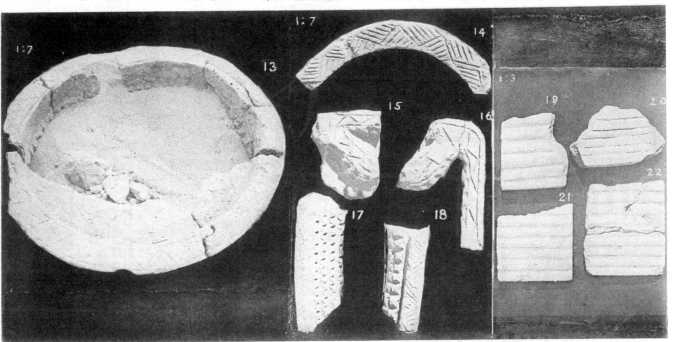

13-18. POTTERY FIRE PLACES AND FRAGMENTS.   19-22. GREEN GLAZED TILING.

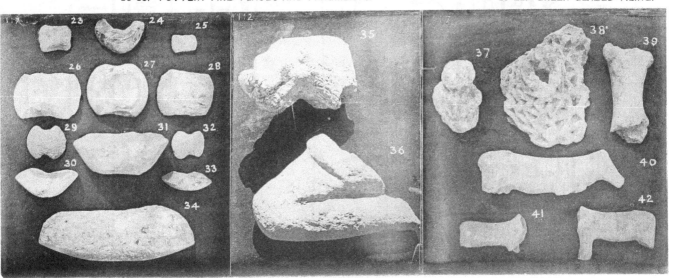

23, 34. STONE VASE GRINDERS.   35, 36. POTTERY FIGURES.   37. STONE FIGURE.   38-42. POTTERY.

1. CLAY SEAL OF SHEPSESKAF.   2. LIMESTONE BASE OF ASSA.

6, 7. RED GRANITE HEAD OF A KING.

8. STELE OF NEKHT.   9. OFFERING SLAB (?) OF USERTESEN I. AND BASE, 10.   3-5. COLUMN OF ANTEF V.

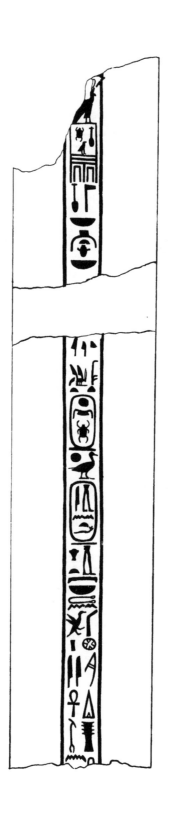

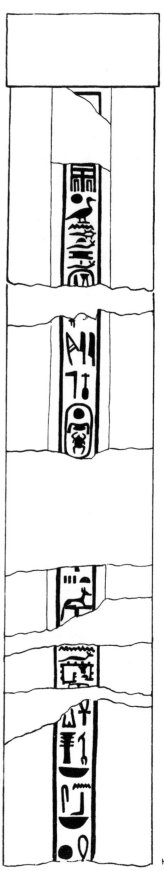

H.P.

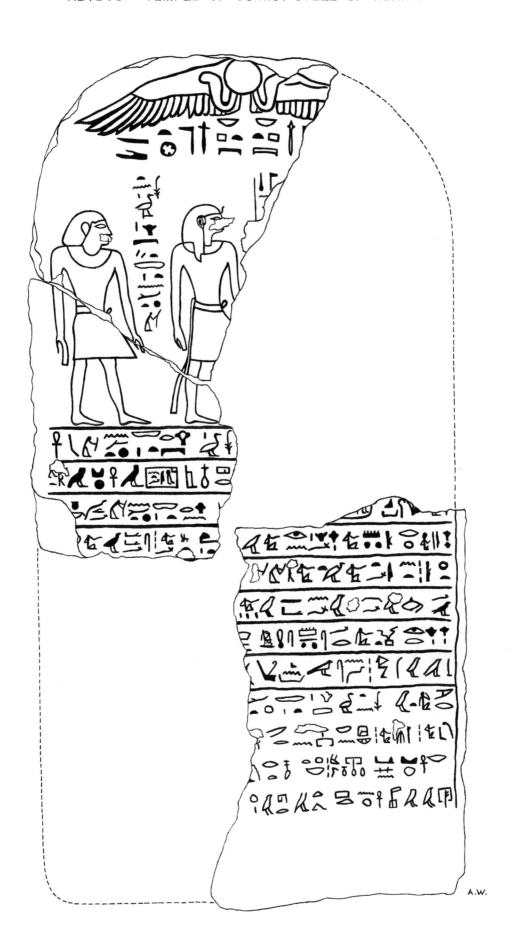

A.W.

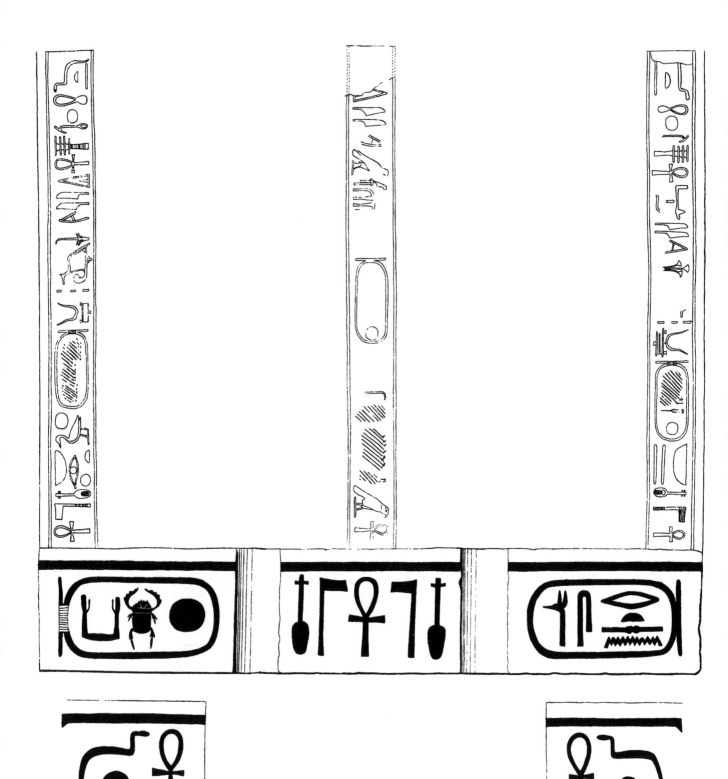

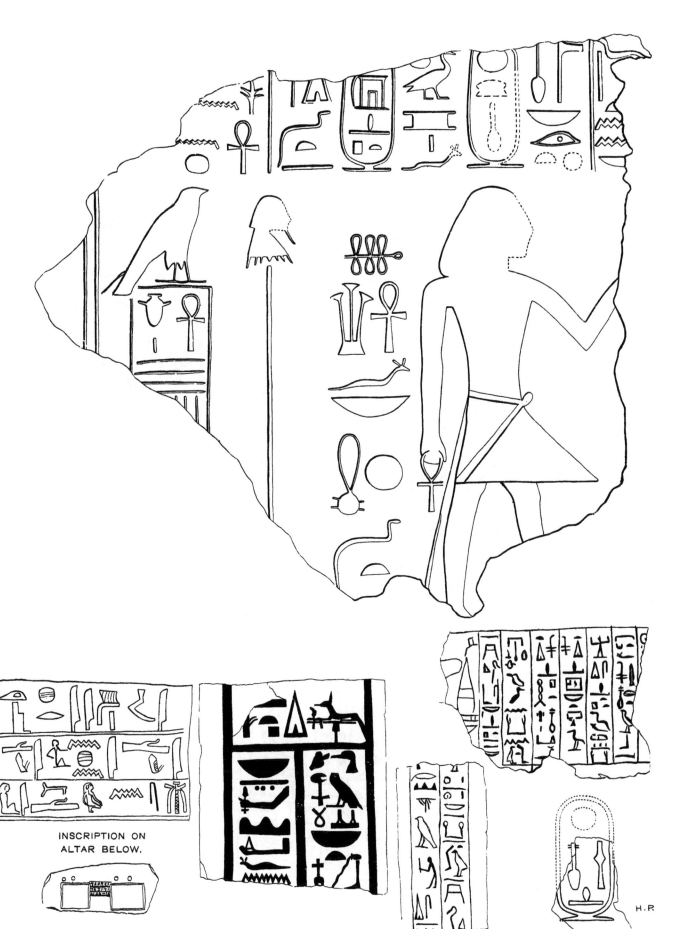

INSCRIPTION ON
ALTAR BELOW.

H. P.

1. SLAB OF TAHUTMES III.   2. LINTEL OF TAHUTMES II. AND III.

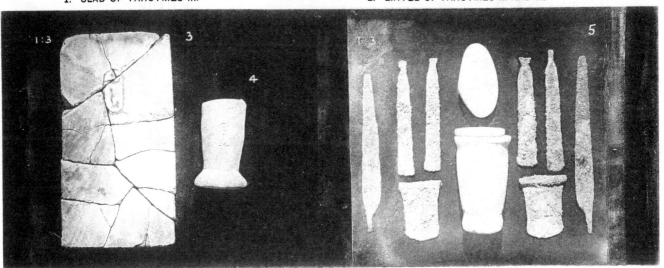

FOUNDATION DEPOSITS.

3. GREEN GLAZE.   4. LIMESTONE, AMENHOTEP III.   5. MODEL TOOLS, VASE, &c., TAHUTMES III.

6. SLAB OF INSCRIPTION.   7. JASPER HEAD.   8. STEATITE HEAD.   9. BLUE GLASS FISH.

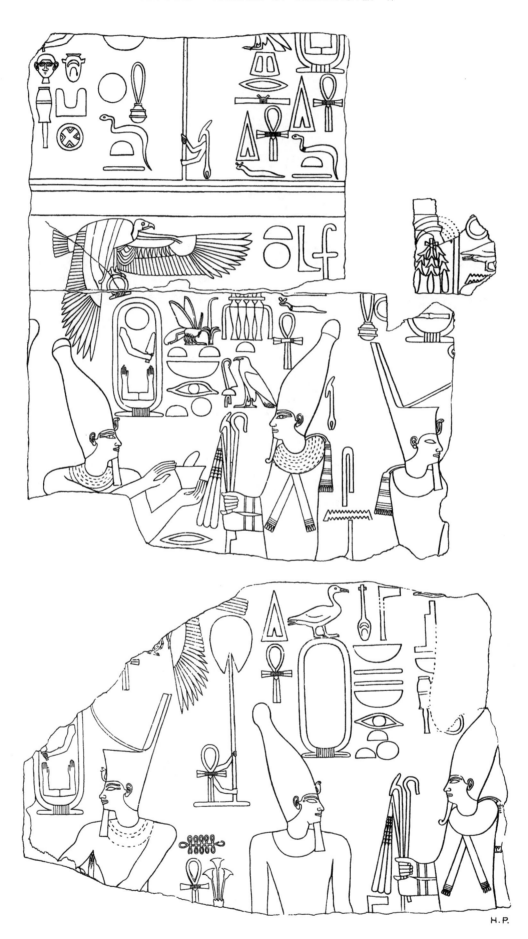

H.P.

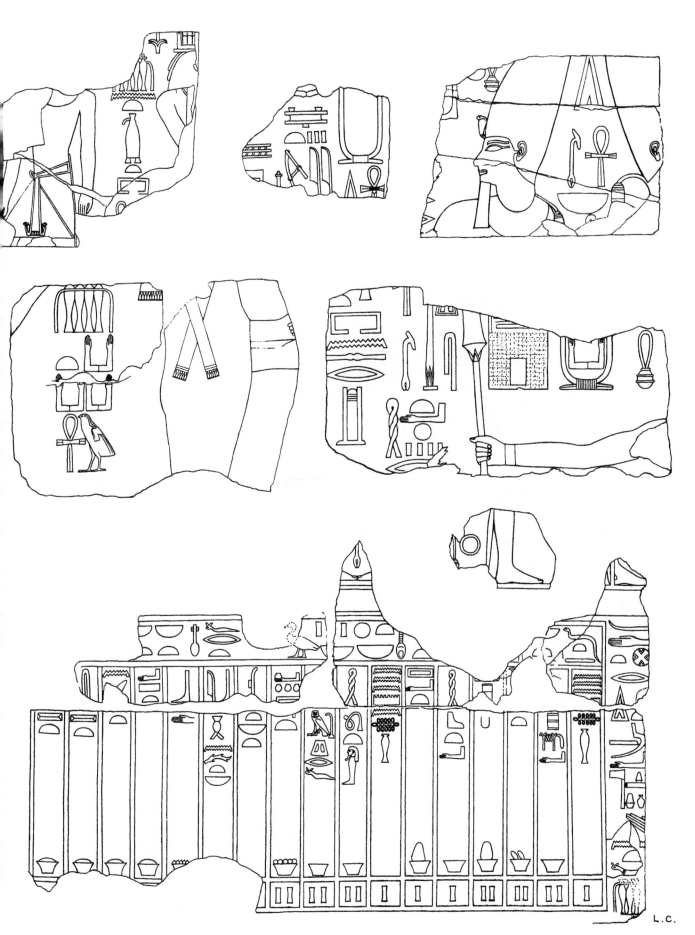

L.C.

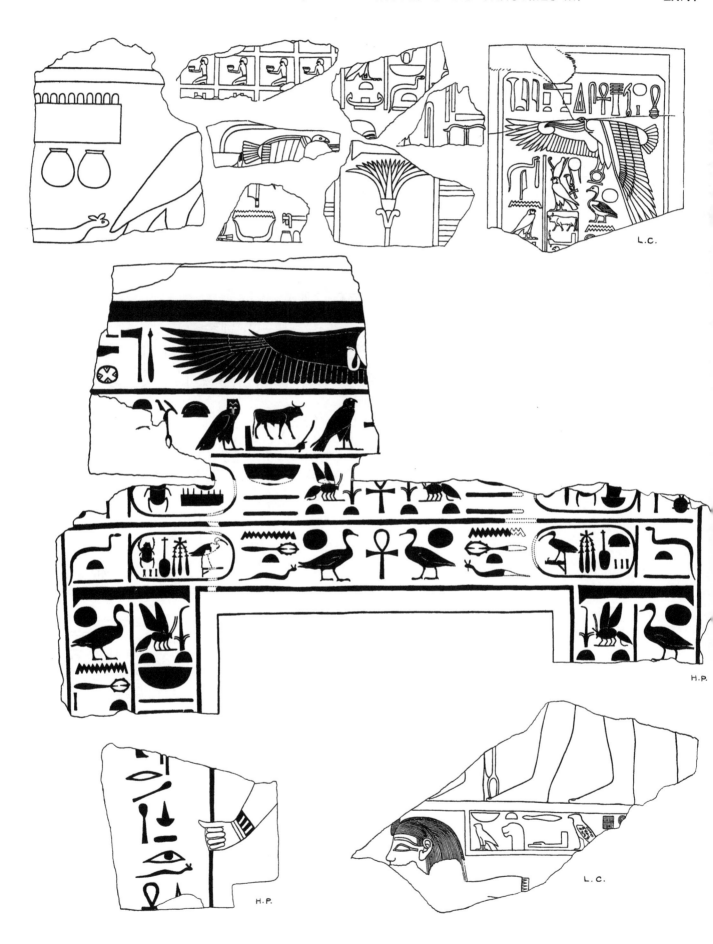

1. FRAGMENTS OF STATUES. 2-4. LIMESTONE STATUE OF PTAHEMUA.

5-7. BACK AND HEAD OF GRANITE FIGURE OF UN-NEFER.

8. LIMESTONE FIGURE OF UN-NEFER. 9, 10. UN-NEFER AND TIY, GRANITE. 11. STELE OF KHAY.

A.W.

H.P.

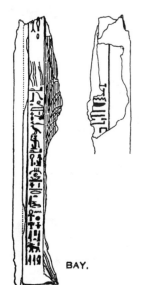

BAY.

URMAAU.

UNNEFER.

UNNEFER.

MENTUEMHAT.

A.W.

MENTUEMHAT.

L.C.

H.P

1—3. BRONZE FIGURES.   4, 5. PORTRAIT HEAD IN QUARTZITE SANDSTONE.

6, 8, 9. FOUNDATION DEPOSITS OF APRIES : 7. OF AAHMES.   10. ALTAR OF AAHMES.

11. DEPOSIT OF NEKHTNEBEF (?).   12—14. STATUES OF AGE OF NEKHTHORHEB.

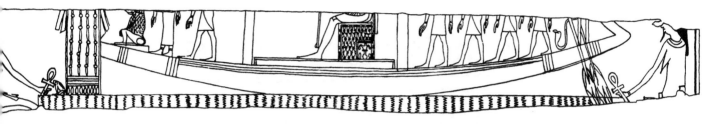

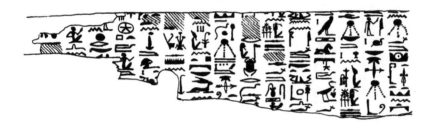

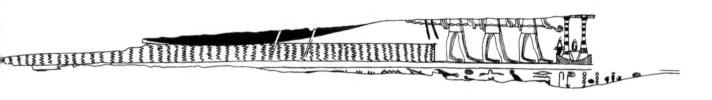

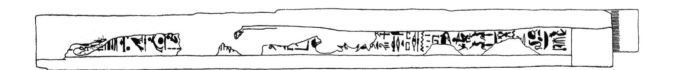

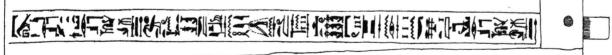

H.P.

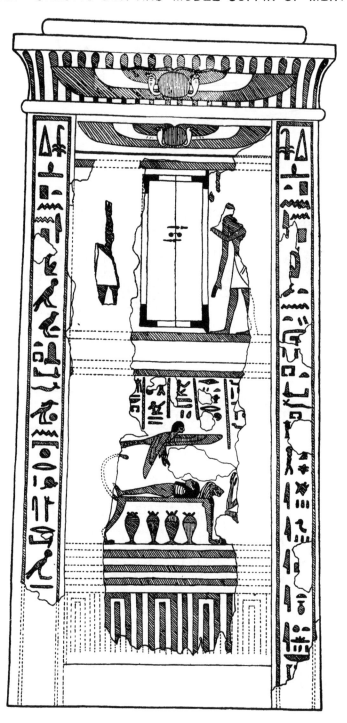

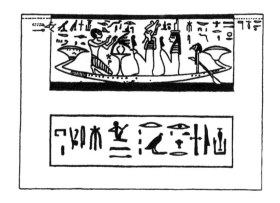

BOX OF TASENMEHT, G 57.

MERTI-HERU

FIGURE OF NUT.

COFFIN OF
TAY-NEKHT. G 57c.

COFFIN OF
MERTI-HERU, G 57a.

COFFIN OF
HERU-MAKHERU
G 57b.

COFFIN OF
MERT-TEFNUT.
G 57d.

GILT
CARTONNAGE
OF
NEB-TA-AHIT,
G 50d.

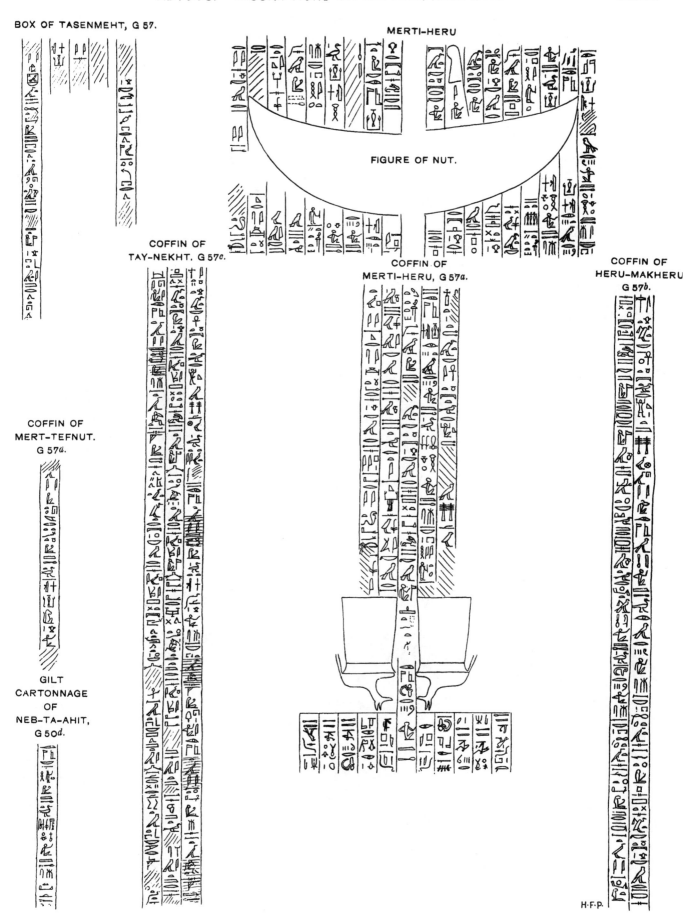

H·F·P.

1, 2. MODEL COFFIN OF MERTIHERU.   3. MODEL COFFIN OF HERU.

4—7. WOODEN CANOPIC BOX OF MERTITEF.

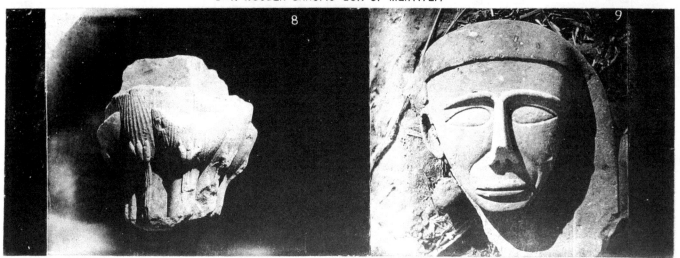

8. LIMESTONE MODEL CAPITAL.   9. HEAD OF PTOLEMAIC SANDSTONE COFFIN.

HAPI-MEN.

NEFERT-IUT.

PEDU-EN-AST.

HOR-UZA.

H.P.

H·P.

G 50 D

G 50 C

H.P.

ORDER AS FOUND.

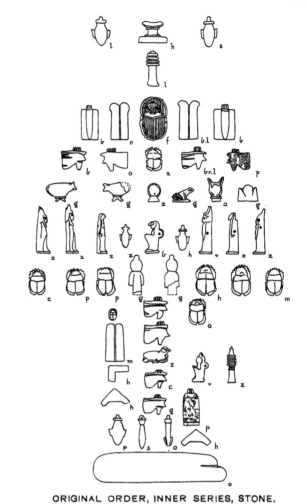

ORIGINAL ORDER, INNER SERIES, STONE.

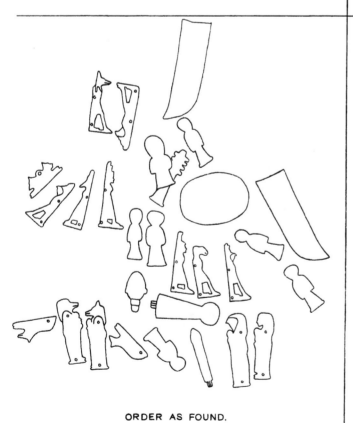

ORDER AS FOUND.

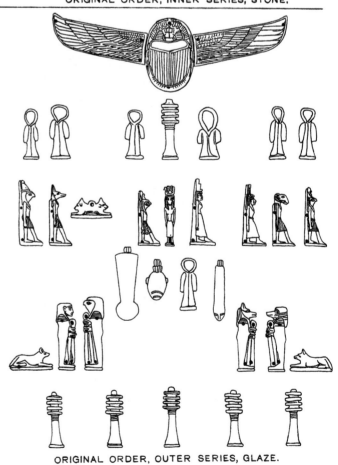

ORIGINAL ORDER, OUTER SERIES, GLAZE.

1. BLUE GLAZED USHABTIS OF ZEDHER.

2. BLUE USHABTIS OF PEDUASAR, SON OF ZEDHER.

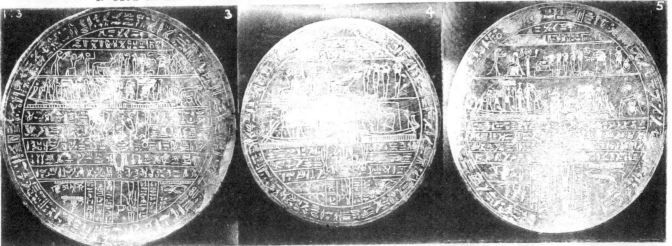

3. BRONZE HYPOCEPHALUS OF ZEDHER: 4, 5. OF THE FAMILY OF ZEDHER.

8. BEAD FRINGE OF HAPI-MEN.

6. COFFIN OF IMHOTEP.

7. COFFIN OF HERUZA.

9. FOOTCASE AND PECTORAL OF HAPI-MEN.

10. CORNER OF DOMED TOMB.

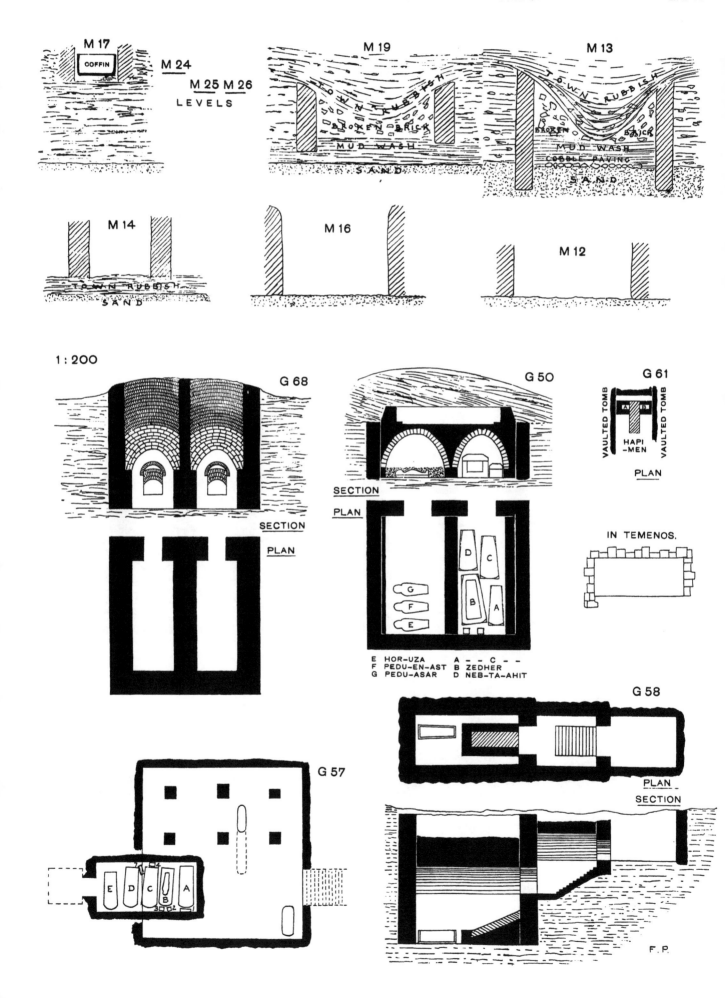

M 17

COFFIN

M 24

M 25 M 26

LEVELS

M 19

TOWN RUBBISH

BROKEN BRICK

MUD WASH

SAND

M 13

TOWN RUBBISH

BROKEN BRICK

MUD WASH

COBBLE PAVING

SAND

M 14

TOWN RUBBISH

SAND

M 16

M 12

1:200

G 68

SECTION

PLAN

G 50

SECTION

PLAN

D C

G

F B A

E

E HOR-UZA   A -- C --
F PEDU-EN-AST   B ZEDHER
G PEDU-ASAR   D NEB-TA-AHIT

G 61

VAULTED TOMB   A B   VAULTED TOMB

HAPI-MEN

PLAN

IN TEMENOS.

G 58

PLAN

SECTION

G 57

E D C A
B

F. P.

For EU product safety concerns, contact us at Calle de José Abascal, 56–1°,
28003 Madrid, Spain or eugpsr@cambridge.org.